7

Fourth Edition

by Jonathan D. Kantrowitz

Edited by Katherine Pierpont

Class Pack ISBN: 978-0-7827-1019-9 • Student Book ISBN: 978-0-7827-1006-9
Item Code QWK1086

Queue, Inc. • 80 Hathaway Drive, Stratford, CT 06615
(800) 232-2224 • Fax: (800) 775-2729 • www.qworkbooks.com

Table of Contents

To the Students

Tips for Answering Multiple-Choice Questions

Multiple-choice questions have a stem, which is a question or an incomplete sentence, followed by four answer choices. You should select only one answer choice. The following are some tips to help you correctly answer multiple-choice questions on standardized tests:

- Read each passage carefully.
- Read each question and think about the answer. You may look back to the reading selection as often as necessary.
- For each question, choose the best answer, and completely fill in the circle in the space provided on your answer sheet.
- If you do not know the answer to a question, skip it and go on. You may return to it later if you have time.
- If you finish the section of the test that you are working on early, you may review your answers in that section only. Don't go on to the next section of the test.

Tips for Answering Open-Response Questions

In this book, students will also be asked to answer open-response questions once they have finished reading some of the passages. Open-response items allow the students to practice their writing skills by answering questions about a passage in their own words.

Remember to:

- Read the question carefully. Be sure you understand it before you begin writing.
- Be sure your essay has a main idea. This should be in your introduction.
- Support your main idea with details, explanations, and examples.
- State your ideas in a clear sequence.
- Include an opening and a closing.
- Use a variety of words and vary your sentence structure.
- Check your spelling, capitalization, and punctuation.
- Write neatly.

from "THE LIGHTHOUSE"

by Henry Wadsworth Longfellow

The rocky ledge runs far into the sea,
And on its outer point, some miles away,
The lighthouse lifts its massive masonry,
A pillar of fire by night, of cloud by day.

Even at this distance I can see the tides,
Upheaving, break unheard along its base,
A speechless wrath, that rises and subsides
In the white lip and tremor of the face.

And as the evening darkens, lo! how bright,
Through the deep purple of the twilight air,
Beams forth the sudden radiance of its light
With strange, unearthly splendor in the glare!

Not one alone; from each projecting cape
And perilous reef along the ocean's verge,
Starts into life a dim, gigantic shape,
Holding its lantern o'er the restless surge. . . .

And the great ships sail outward and return,
Bending and bowing o'er the billowy swells,
And ever joyful, as they see it burn,
They wave their silent welcomes and farewells.

They come forth from the darkness, and their sails
Gleam for a moment only in the blaze,
And eager faces, as the light unveils,
Gaze at the tower, and vanish while they gaze.

The mariner remembers when a child,
On his first voyage, he saw it fade and sink;
And when, returning from adventures wild,
He saw it rise again o'er ocean's brink.

Steadfast, serene, immovable, the same
Year after year, through all the silent night
Burns on forevermore that quenchless flame,
Shines on that inextinguishable light! . . .

The startled waves leap over it; the storm
Smites it with all the scourges of the rain,
And steadily against its solid form
Press the great shoulders of the hurricane. . . .

"Sail on!" it says, "sail on, ye stately ships!
And with your floating bridge the ocean span;
Be mine to guard this light from all eclipse,
Be yours to bring man nearer unto man!"

1. The author's **main** purpose for writing the poem is to

A. describe the color of twilight.
B. honor a special lighthouse.
C. persuade readers to be sailors.
D. explain the return of a sailboat.

Answer choice A is incorrect because, although Longfellow says that the twilight is purple, that is not the central purpose of the poem. Answer choice B looks like a good answer because the poem is about a lighthouse guiding ships around reefs and a storm. Answer choice C is incorrect because the author does not address the reader directly. Answer choice D is incorrect because the poem is more focused on the lighthouse than on a boat. Answer choice B is the correct answer.

2. What happens after the storm hits the lighthouse?

A. The storm floods the lighthouse and washes most of it out to sea.
B. The sailors give up hope that the lighthouse can lead them to safety.
C. The lighthouse survives the storm and its lamp continues to shine.
D. The lighthouse lamp goes out, but is quickly relit to guide the ships.

Answer choice A is incorrect because the lighthouse calls out to the ships; it could not have been destroyed. Answer choice B is incorrect because the sailors don't appear to change their attitudes because of the storm hitting the lighthouse. Answer choice C appears to be correct because the lighthouse does tell the ships to sail on. Answer choice D is incorrect because the lighthouse is meant to guard against an eclipse (i.e., any loss of light). Answer choice C is the correct answer.

3. Which word **best** describes the lighthouse?

A. mysterious
B. reliable
C. beautiful
D. run-down

Reread the poem to see which word best describes the lighthouse. From the way the author describes the lighthouse, it is more predictable than mysterious (answer choice A). It is reliable; in the eighth stanza of the poem, the author describes the lighthouse as "steadfast" and "immovable" and says the lighthouse is the same year after year. This is a good answer choice. The lighthouse is probably beautiful, but answer choice B is a better answer. The author does not imply that the lighthouse is rundown. Answer choice B is the best answer.

4. The word <u>smites</u> probably means

   A. assists.
   B. bypasses.
   C. beckons.
   D. strikes.

   Answer choice A is incorrect because the storm brings danger, not assistance, to the lighthouse. Answer choice B is incorrect because the storm and the lighthouse seem to collide with, rather than to avoid, each other. Answer choice C is incorrect because there does not seem to be any communication between the storm and the lighthouse. Answer choice D is correct because the storm attacks the lighthouse with "scourges of the rain."

5. In the fourth line, the author uses the phrase "pillar of fire" in order to

   A. explain how dangerous the lighthouses can be.
   B. describe how tall the lighthouse is up close.
   C. show how bright the lighthouse is at night.
   D. explain how comforting the lighthouse is to sailors.

   In line 4, the author calls the lighthouse "a pillar of fire by night." This suggests that, like a fire burning in the darkness, a lighthouse is bright and gives off a lot of light at night. Answer choice A is incorrect because the author never mentions that the lighthouse can be dangerous. Answer choice B is incorrect because the phrase "pillar of fire" has nothing to do with the height of the lighthouse. Answer choice C is a good answer. The phrase "pillar of fire" does help to show how bright the lighthouse is at night. Answer choice D is incorrect because while the lighthouse is a comfort to sailors, this phrase from the poem does not convey that message. Answer choice C is the best answer.

6. How does the author feel about the lighthouse? Identify and explain two details from the poem in your answer.

You have to write out your answer to this question. Begin by rereading the poem and looking for clues as to how the author feels about the lighthouse. For example, in the third stanza, the author says that the lighthouse is very bright. He uses exclamation points to show that he is excited about this brightness. In the fifth stanza, he says that the people and ships are joyful when they see the lighthouse.

Based on these details, you might write an answer like this:

The author seems to value the lighthouse because of its brightness. For example, in the third stanza of the poem, he says that the lighthouse "Beams forth the sudden radiance of it light / With strange, unearthly splendor in the glare!" He seems to think that the glare from the lighthouse for those who see it is splendid and wonderful. He uses exclamation points to show that he is excited about this brightness.

Also, in the fifth stanza, he says that the people and ships are joyful when they see the lighthouse.

The people are joyful when they see the lighthouse because
That means shore is nearby
The author Thinks the Lighthouse as hope in darkness
as it guides all boats away to safty.

THE WONDERS OF WEATHER

As the school bus continued down the road, Michael rested his head in his hands. There wasn't a cloud in the sky on this warm spring day. It was the first nice day of the season and Michael wished that he was outside playing baseball. Instead, he was on a class trip to the local TV station. There, the students would learn about meteorology, the study of weather, from the head of the department. While he enjoyed the idea of being out of the classroom, Michael wasn't thrilled about spending this beautiful day trapped indoors.

As he exited the bus, Michael noticed that many of his fellow classmates actually seemed excited about this excursion. This baffled Michael, who couldn't understand what was so interesting about weather. To Michael, all that weather people did was to tell you whether or not you needed a jacket and most of the time it seemed like they were guessing. Before heading inside, Michael took one more longing look at the bright sunshine and wished that he could stay outdoors.

The class was immediately greeted by a man with a big smile and an abnormal necktie. Michael recognized him as Andy Todd, the local weather forecaster. Mr. Todd took the class inside the weather department where dozens of complicated-looking instruments hummed and flashed. Michael wondered what purpose all of these machines served.

After Mr. Todd said that he would be happy to answer any questions that the students might have, a bunch of kids raised their hands. Michael thought that many of the questions were pretty boring. One girl asked what caused thunder and another wanted to know how rainbows formed.

Michael's teacher was encouraging every student in the class to ask a question and soon he was the only student who hadn't said a word. After a slight pause, he asked, "How do you predict the weather?"

"I was hoping someone would ask that question," exclaimed Mr. Todd. His smile grew larger as he started explaining the different methods that were used for predicting weather.

The first method Mr. Todd introduced was the Persistence Method. Mr. Todd explained that meteorologists would look at today's weather and assume that very little would change from one day to the next.

"But isn't that like guessing?" asked Michael.

Mr. Todd agreed that the Persistence Method worked best in areas where the weather was fairly consistent. For example, southern California's weather varies little on a day-to-day basis, making it easier to know what tomorrow will bring. This method didn't account for unusual weather patterns that might occur. In Michael's mind, this didn't seem like a very reliable system.

Next, Mr. Todd explained climatology, the study of climates. Weather forecasters look at years of records to predict what the weather will be like on a certain day. If a meteorologist is trying to predict the weather for June 14th in New York City, he or she will look at what the weather there was like in years past on the same date. If the average weather for that date has been warm with no precipitation, then the forecaster would predict that the same will be true this year. Michael didn't think that this method sounded much better than the previous one.

Finally, Mr. Todd introduced the Trends Method, the system that he used to predict the local forecast. Satellites in outer space send messages alerting meteorologists about storm patterns in other parts of the world. With this information, Mr. Todd uses mathematics to figure out how, where, and when a weather system might move. For instance, if a storm is coming in from the west at a certain speed, the meteorologist can accurately approximate how long it will take for that storm to move into the area.

This method is often used to help prepare people for severe weather conditions. Michael still seemed doubtful, so Mr. Todd offered to prove himself. On the computer, Mr. Todd showed the class a map of the country. Mr. Todd showed them a storm system that was moving east. He explained that the storm was five hundred miles away, moving about two hundred fifty miles a day. By dividing the distance away from the storm by how fast it was moving, Mr. Todd showed the class that they could predict that the storm would arrive at its destination in about two days.

"I made this prediction two days ago, which means that this storm should be moving into our area just about now."

Michael raised his eyebrows in surprise. Half an hour ago he'd been looking at a cloudless sky! He didn't believe that the weather could have changed so drastically in such a short amount of time.

Suddenly, there was a rumble from outside. The students crowded around the window. Large, black clouds had rolled in and there were flashes of lightning in the distance. Michael couldn't believe his eyes! He looked over at a smiling Mr. Todd. He was now convinced that there was more to meteorology than he'd originally thought.

1. Which of these choices **best** summarizes the story?

A. Michael goes on a class trip to the local TV station. There, he meets Mr. Todd, the local weather man. Michael listens to several of his classmates ask questions about the weather. He finally figures out that meteorology is not very accurate.
B. Michael goes on a class trip to the TV station. There, he learns about meteorology from Mr. Todd, the local weather man. Mr. Todd explains several different ways to predict the weather. After Mr. Todd accurately predicts a storm, Michael realizes that meteorology really is interesting.
C. Michael learns about meteorology one day. He becomes so interested in the different ways that meteorologists predict weather that he decides to get more information on meteorology.
D. Michael goes on a class trip to the TV station. Michael feels bored during trip. He doesn't believe that weather can change quickly or that Mr. Todd can predict a storm two days in advance. Michael decides to go outside to enjoy the weather, only to get caught in the rain.

Each of these answer choices includes some correct information from the story. However, the question asks you to choose the one that provides the best summary of the whole story. Answer choice A includes true statements, but it leaves out the important part of the story in which Michael learns that meteorology is interesting. Answer choice C omits the information about Mr. Todd, who is an important character in this story. Answer choice D also does not include a full summary of the story. Answer choice B is best. It describes each of the most important events of the story.

2. According to the story, which method could **best** predict a severe thunderstorm?

A. the Trends Method
B. the Persistence Method
C. the Climatologic Method
D. the California Method

This question asks you to draw a conclusion about the information in the story. If you don't know the answer to this question, you can find it by rereading the story. The story says that the Trends Method (answer choice A) is the best method to predict severe weather. The Persistence Method (answer choice B) and the Climatology Method (answer choice C) are not the best for this. The California Method (answer choice D) is not mentioned in the passage; only the *state* of California is mentioned. Answer choice A is the correct answer.

3. In the third paragraph, the word abnormal probably means

A. flimsy.
B. unusual.
C. accessible.
D. colossal.

To answer this question, think about the prefix *ab-*. It means "not." Therefore, the man's tie was not normal. *Flimsy* (answer choice A) means "not sturdy." *Unusual* (answer choice B) is a good answer—something that is *unusual* is not normal. Answer choice C is not correct because *accessible* means "within reach." *Colossal* (answer choice D) means "huge" and his necktie probably wasn't all that big. Answer choice B is the best answer.

4. Why does Michael think the persistence method is unreliable?

A. It does not predict unusual weather.
B. It is based on weather from years past.
C. It has only been used for a short time.
D. It needs messages from satellites in space.

To find the answer to this question, go back and reread the part about the persistence method. The passage says that this method works best in areas where the weather is fairly consistent. Michael thinks this method is unreliable because it doesn't predict unusual weather (answer choice A). This method is not based on weather from years past (answer choice B) and the passage doesn't say it has only been in use for a short time (answer choice C). And this is not the method that relies on messages from satellites in space (answer choice D). Answer choice A is the correct answer.

5. Which words **best** describe Mr. Todd in the story?

A. enthusiastic and likable
B. determined and impatient
C. anxious and skeptical
D. easygoing and popular

This question asks you to choose a pair of words that best describe Mr. Todd. Answer choice A describes Mr. Todd as *enthusiastic* and *likable*. This seems like a good answer choice. Mr. Todd is nice to the students and he is certainly *enthusiastic* about his job. Answer choice B describes Mr. Todd as *determined* and *impatient*. He might be *determined*, but he isn't *impatient*. This is not the best answer choice. He also is not *anxious* or *skeptical* (answer choice C). We don't know for sure that he is *easygoing* or *popular* (answer choice D). Answer choice A is the best answer.

6. The third paragraph is **mainly** about

   A. a warm spring day.
   B. a classroom full of books.
   C. a workplace full of technology.
   D. a group of students smiling.

Each of these answer choices applies to the story in some way, but only one matches the events in the third paragraph. Look back at that paragraph for hints. The story takes place during a warm spring day (answer choice A); however, the students are inside during most of the story. The students left their classroom (answer choice B) before the story began. There was a group of students, and some may have been smiling (answer choice D), but the students aren't the focus of this paragraph. The best answer is answer choice C—the paragraph deals with Mr. Todd's workspace and its many "complicated-looking instruments."

7. Which method of predicting the weather do you think is the **most** interesting? Use details from the story to support your answer.

You have to write out your answer to this question. Before you begin, you need to go back to the story and read about the different methods of predicting the weather. Then choose the one you find the most interesting and explain why.

You might write something like this:

I think the Trends Method of predicting the weather is the most interesting because it uses messages from satellites in outer space. This is fascinating to me and I would like to learn more about this kind of technology. I would really enjoy tracking storms in different parts of the world and then predicting if and when they will come to our area.

Each student's response should be clearly written, based on accurate information, and convincing.

I think the trans method is the most interesting because satalites are tracking clouds unlike the preexisting methbd is a hypothesis of where the cloud is going to end up.

OUR INTERSTATE HIGHWAY SYSTEM

The interstate highway system looks like a series of ribbons strung across the face of the country. Miles of highways link cities and regions together. Upon closer inspection, we can see that the roadways have a distinct pattern. They wander through isolated areas of rural countryside and merge together around large cities. The network of roads, officially called the Dwight D. Eisenhower National System of Interstate and Defense Highways, was designed and built over most of the twentieth century.

Many roads in the 1930s were designed and built before the invention of automobiles. These roads were made of mud or wooden planks and were difficult to use in bad weather. People either walked or used trains to get to many places then. As people began to drive, cars clogged the streets. Travel to and from different cities took a lot of time because the roads were small, twisting, and not built to support the traffic of many heavy cars. Taking a trip to the next town could take several hours, and it took months to drive across the country. People began to discuss how to build a transportation system that would connect the country's largest cities.

Different groups disagreed over who would pay for the roads and how many roads there would be. By the time World War II began, there was still no large highway system in the United States. During the war, Americans began noticing the superhighways in Europe. One of the most famous is the German Autobahn, which has highways designed to connect cities and larger roadways that run all the way across Germany. General Dwight D. Eisenhower saw that his troops could move quickly when they used the network of large roads between major cities. He knew it took a long time to cross the United States. More than two decades earlier, in 1919, Eisenhower had accompanied an army convoy that traveled from Washington, D.C., to San Francisco. The trip, which took 62 days, was difficult because the trucks moved slowly across the small roads between many towns.

After the war, Eisenhower returned to the United States; he was elected president in 1952. He asked Congress to develop and fund a national highway that would stretch across the entire country and connect its largest cities. He thought that this highway could make it easier to move people and equipment from one area to another in an emergency. Highways like these would also let businesses send materials more efficiently and allow thousands of Americans to tour areas of the country that they had never seen before.

In 1956, Congress passed the Interstate Highway and Defense Act, a landmark in the development of the roadway. The law established our current interstate system and required the federal government to pay most of the cost to build and maintain the highways. People then had to build the roads and connect all of the cities. Some of the highways that already existed were turned into interstates while tens of thousands of new miles of roadway were paved to enlarge the network of roads.

Nearly 50,000 miles of interstate highway exist today. The longest interstate is Interstate 90, which runs 3,021 miles from Seattle to Boston. Interstate 95 travels through the largest number of states—16—as it stretches 1,921 miles from Maine to Florida. Both interstates run either the entire length or the entire width of the continental U.S.

These are some other interstates that run across the whole country:

Interstate 10	2,461 miles
Interstate 80	2,900 miles
Interstate 75	1,786 miles
Interstate 35	1,568 miles
Interstate 15	1,434 miles
Interstate 5	1,381 miles
Interstate 55	964 miles
Interstate 65	887 miles

Once the massive highways had been built, Americans realized that they could move outside the city limits. New communities, called suburbs, popped up outside the largest cities, and people moved to these new neighborhoods. People realized that it was easy to use the interstates to drive from the suburbs into the cities. The interstates became filled with large trucks whose drivers take goods from coast to coast. Many of the materials had previously been taken by train, but companies decided that it was easier to ship items using the interstate highways.

The interstates changed the way Americans travel. Thousands of people are now able to take short weekend vacations to other cities, where they can visit relatives, amusement parks, or other attractions. What once took most of a day is now a two-hour drive, and it's possible to drive across a large part of most of the country within one or two days. The interstate system has made it easier to travel throughout regions and across most of the country.

1. The author includes the information in the second paragraph in order to

   A. review how long most trips used to take.
   B. explain why earlier roads were difficult to drive on.
   C. compare the roads and the railroads of the 1930s.
   D. demonstrate why people began driving cars.

Paragraph 2 was not meant to serve to explain how long trips took (answer choice A) or to compare roads with railroads (answer choice C). Also, it does not try to tell what made people want to drive cars (answer choice D). Paragraph 2 shows readers that the roads in the U.S. had become out-of-date (answer choice B). The roads had been built before automobiles were invented and these roads needed to be updated in order to handle a high volume of cars. Answer choice B tells the main purpose of the paragraph.

2. In the fifth paragraph, word <u>landmark</u> probably means

   A. monument.
   B. turning point.
   C. guide book.
   D. instructions.

The word *landmark* has several possible meanings. Answer choice A is not the best, because a *monument* is usually a solid, physical thing. The passage doesn't seem to be talking about a physical thing here. Answer choice C is not correct, because there is no mention of a guide to the highway system. For the same reason, *instructions* (answer choice D) is probably not right. In the passage, the word *landmark* refers to a major turning point in the history of highways. Answer choice B is best.

3. According to the passage, why was travel between cities difficult for early drivers?

   A. Early drivers did not know how to operate automobiles very well.
   B. The small roads had not been designed for automobile travel.
   C. People did not have maps to help them get from city to city.
   D. The cars were not designed to run for long periods of time.

This question asks about a detail that is discussed in the passage. The passage does not mention that early drivers might have had trouble operating automobiles so, while this may be true, answer choice A is not the correct answer. Does the passage mention that roads were small and not designed for automobile travel (answer choice B)? This fact is discussed in the passage; it may be the correct answer. The passage does not mention that maps did not exist, so answer choice C cannot be correct. While the passage does mention that the trucks in Eisenhower's army convoy trip traveled slowly, it does not discuss the length of time cars were able to run during trips, so answer choice D is also incorrect. The best answer is answer choice B.

4. How did highways help the development of suburbs in the United States?

A. They made it possible for people to live outside of cities.
B. They helped businesses move goods around the country.
C. They shortened driving time for everyone in the country.
D. They showed people that these communities existed.

Answer choice A suggests that highways made it possible for people to live outside of cities. This detail is mentioned in the passage and is a possible explanation for the development of suburbs, so it may be the correct answer. However, read the other answer choices before choosing answer choice A. The passage does mention that highways helped businesses move goods around the country (answer choice B), and it also discusses the fact that highways shortened driving time for Americans (answer choice C), but neither of these details from the passage explains how highways helped suburbs to develop, so neither is the correct answer. Highways could not have showed people that suburbs existed (answer choice D) because suburbs did not exist until after the highways were created. The correct answer is A.

5. Which interstate runs for 1,568 miles?

A. Interstate 90
B. Interstate 35
C. Interstate 95
D. Interstate 80

This question asks you to identify a detail in the passage. Look carefully at the list of interstates and their distances. It lists several highways, including Interstate 90 (answer choice A), Interstate 35 (answer choice B), Interstate 95 (answer choice C), and Interstate 80 (answer choice D). By looking at the list, you will find that only answer choice B, Interstate 35, runs for 1,568 miles. That is the correct answer.

6. Read the sentence below from the passage.

They wander through isolated areas of rural countryside and <u>merge</u> together around large cities.

In the sentence, the word <u>merge</u> probably means

A. pull.
B. mix.
C. join.
D. move.

Merge does not mean pull (answer choice A). The highways system also does not mix the countryside and large cities (answer choice B) or move them together (answer choice D). The highway system does join the two places together (answer choice C). Answer choice C is correct.

7. The author compares interstate highways to ribbons in order to show that interstates

A. are laid out in large loops.
B. were made when people wore ribbons.
C. tie together the parts of the country.
D. are known for their beauty.

Answer choice A is not the best. Some interstates may travel in loops, but most are designed in long lines. The passage never mentions ribbons or clothing (answer choice B), so that is not the right answer. Also, the passage focuses more on the usefulness of the interstates instead of on their appearance (answer choice D), so that is also incorrect. The best choice is answer choice C; interstates are like ribbons because they tie the country together.

8. Think about the effect that the highway system has had on our country. Describe what you think the country might be like if we didn't have the highway system. How would this affect people's lives? Use details from the passage to support your answer.

You have to write out your answer to this question. Before you begin, go back to the passage and read about how the country operated before the highway system was put into place. Then, think about how different our country might be without it.

You might write something like this:

One possible response:

Without the highway system, our country would not be as connected as it is today. It would be much more difficult for people to travel from one state to another. Families would probably not see each other as often as they do now. It would be much harder for businesses to have offices in different states. Without a highway system, it would be very difficult for people to live outside of the cities where they work. People's lives would be very different today if we did not have the highway system.

without highways cities would expand slower. Adding to that gocerie would be less fress and the city won't be advanced as today

HOW TO MAKE A PINHOLE CAMERA

Today, there are dozens of cameras that allow you to view your pictures almost instantly. These complicated machines are great for snapping pictures, but can't really explain how a camera converts a large scene into a small picture. An easy way to learn more about basic camera functions is to build a pinhole camera.

A pinhole camera is a small, light-proof container with a pinhole that acts as a lens. Like the shutter on a normal camera, the pinhole allows only a small amount of light to pass through while the photo is being taken. The small size of the pinhole reduces the speed at which light travels, in the same way that the glass of a camera lens does. The slowing down of light is what allows cameras to capture an image.

The pinhole camera faces the scene that you want to take a picture of. Each point in the scene transmits light, which passes through the pinhole. This light projects the image onto the other end of the container where it is inverted and reversed. At this end, a small square of regular film is secured to capture the image.

Because the pinhole is smaller than a lens, which would allow more light to pass into the camera in a short amount of time, the picture takes longer to develop on the film. Despite this, building this camera is a fun way to learn about the principles of picture-taking. All you need are some basic materials that you might already have laying around your house and some patience to build your own working camera.

Materials You Will Need:

- a clean, cylindrical oatmeal container
- flat, black paint
- black electrical tape
- black paper
- clear adhesive tape
- a needle
- scissors
- camera film

Steps for Making a Pinhole Camera

1. The first thing you need to do is to make sure that your container is completely light-proof. Light inside the container could ruin your picture. Coat the inside, outside, and lid of your oatmeal container with black paint. Allow the paint to dry completely. If there are any seams on the outside of the container, cover them with black electrical tape.
2. Ask an adult to help you put a hole with a needle into the end of the container that doesn't open. The best way to do this is to twist the needle back and forth instead of pushing the needle right through the lid. This will make sure that the hole is small and precise, ensuring that your pictures will be sharp.
3. Use your scissors to cut a square smaller than the width of the lid out of the black piece of paper. This will be your camera's shutter, which prevents light from getting into the camera through the pinhole when you aren't taking a picture. Use the clear adhesive tape to attach the square on one side, so that the other side can still be moved to snap a photo.
4. This next step needs to be done in complete darkness to make sure that the film is not exposed. You might want to get a special safelight bulb at a local camera shop so you can see in the dark. Use the scissors to cut out a square of camera film. Attach the edges of the film to the container's lid using the clear adhesive tape.
5. Now you're ready to start taking pictures with your homemade camera! Keep in mind that pinhole cameras work best when used outdoors on a sunny day. Also remember to keep the camera very still so that your picture doesn't blur. After you've finished taking pictures, you can take your film to a local photo shop to be processed.

1. In the fourth paragraph, the word <u>develop</u> probably means

   A. establish.
   B. grow.
   C. improve.
   D. form.

For this question, you need to identify how the word *develop* is being used in the context of the sentence. Answer choices A, B, C, and D all contain definitions of the word *develop*. *Develop* can mean "establish," "improve," "grow," or "form." Your challenge is to decide what the word means in the context of this particular sentence. In this sentence, *develop* refers to how long it takes the picture to form. The best choice is answer choice D.

2. The author includes the information in the first paragraph in order to

A. list the materials that are needed to make a pinhole camera.
B. explain what pinhole cameras are and how they work.
C. explain how and where you can take pictures with a camera.
D. list the steps to follow when building your own pinhole camera.

Think about what you learned from the first paragraph. If you don't remember, you can look back to the passage to refresh your memory. This paragraph does not list materials (answer choice A), since that is done later in the passage. Details of how and where you can take pictures (answer choice C) are given later, as is the list of assembly steps (answer choice D). Paragraph 1 introduces pinhole cameras and tells how they operate (answer choice B).

3. Why should the reader perform step 4 in the dark?

A. so the film will not become blurry
B. so the film will develop quickly
C. so the film will not be ruined by the light
D. so the film will stay securely in the camera

This question asks you about a detail in one of the steps listed in the passage. Read step 4 again. According to the passage, you should do step 4 in the dark so you do not expose the film. Exposing the film would ruin it. Answer choice C is the correct answer.

4. In the first paragraph, the word <u>converts</u> probably means

A. discards.
B. mangles.
C. proposes.
D. transforms.

The word *converts* means "transforms." By looking at the other words in the sentence, the reader can see that the author is talking about how a camera changes or transforms a large scene into a small picture. *Discards* (answer choice A) means "throws away," *mangles* (answer choice B) means "destroys," and *proposes* (answer choice C) means "offers." None of these choices fits in the sentence. The correct answer is answer choice D, *transforms*.

5. What should readers do after they check the container for seams?

A. Paint the container.
B. Ask an adult for help.
C. Cut out a small square.
D. Attach the film inside.

Readers should be painting the container before they check for seams (answer choice A). They do need to ask an adult for help with the needle after checking for seams (answer choice B). The readers should not be cutting out a small square (answer choice C) or attaching the film (answer choice D) after they check for seams; these steps come later. The best choice is answer choice B.

6. What might readers want to purchase at a local camera shop?

A. black and white film
B. safety scissors
C. a camera lens
D. a safelight bulb

The author does not tell readers that they need black and white film (answer choice A) or safety scissors (answer choice B). Readers do not have to purchase a camera lens (answer choice C) because the pinhole acts as a lens. The author does tell readers that they might want to get a safelight bulb (answer choice D) at the shop so that they can see as they are performing step 4.

7. The author says that making a pinhole camera can help the reader to understand photography. Do you think that the information about building a pinhole camera helps the reader to better understand how pictures are taken? Why or why not? Identify and explain two reasons that support your response.

You have to write out your answer to this question. Think carefully before you begin to write your answer. What does the pinhole camera teach you about photography and how pictures are taken? If you need to, go back and reread the passage to help you answer the question.

You might write something like this:

One possible response:

I think that building the pinhole camera helps readers to understand the basic principles of photography. By getting them involved in the process, it lets them see how cameras capture images. Today's digital cameras make taking pictures very easy, but they don't really give you a good idea of how a picture forms in the camera. The pinhole cameras help readers to do this.

Building this will help unerstand how now in day cameras work. This is complicated to describe, so building it will make the crystal crearer

from "A LITTLE PRINCESS" - Part I

by Frances Hodgson Burnett

Once on a dark winter's day, when the yellow fog hung so thick and heavy in the streets of London that the lamps were lighted and the shop windows blazed with gas as they do at night, an odd-looking little girl sat in a cab with her father and was driven rather slowly through the big thoroughfares.

She sat with her feet tucked under her, and leaned against her father, who held her in his arm, as she stared out of the window at the passing people with a queer old-fashioned thoughtfulness in her big eyes.

She was such a little girl that one did not expect to see such a look on her small face. It would have been an old look for a child of twelve, and Sara Crewe was only seven. The fact was, however, that she was always dreaming and thinking odd things and could not herself remember any time when she had not been thinking things about grown-up people and the world they belonged to. She felt as if she had lived a long, long time.

At this moment she was remembering the voyage she had just made from Bombay with her father, Captain Crewe. She was thinking of the big ship, of the Lascars[1] passing silently to and fro on it, of the children playing about on the hot deck, and of some young officers' wives who used to try to make her talk to them and laugh at the things she said.

Principally, she was thinking of what a queer thing it was that at one time one was in India in the blazing sun, and then in the middle of the ocean, and then driving in a strange vehicle through strange streets where the day was as dark as the night. She found this so puzzling that she moved closer to her father.

"Papa," she said in a low, mysterious little voice which was almost a whisper, "papa."

"What is it, darling?" Captain Crewe answered, holding her closer and looking down into her face. "What is Sara thinking of?"

"Is this the place?" Sara whispered, cuddling still closer to him. "Is it, papa?"

"Yes, little Sara, it is. We have reached it at last." And though she was only seven years old, she knew that he felt sad when he said it.

[1] The Lascars are native East Indian seamen.

1. Which statement **best** describes Sara?

~~A.~~ Sara was always getting in trouble.
(B.) Sara was young, but mature.
C. Sara was smart, but very lazy.
D. Sara was very bored by her father.

2. Why did Sara **probably** move close to her father?

(A.) She was overwhelmed by the things she saw.
~~B.~~ She feared that the people would attack her.
~~C.~~ She was cold from the damp London air.
D. She wanted him to tell her more about India.

3. In the first paragraph, the word <u>thoroughfares</u> probably means

~~A.~~ days.
(B.) streets.
~~C.~~ cabs.
~~D.~~ cities.

4. Why do you think Captain Crewe is sad? Use details from the story to support your answer.

I think Captain Crewe was sad ~~bec~~ because in the end of part one it said that She knew he felt sad when he said it. That probably means that when The dad was talking ~~they~~ he sounded sad maybe something bad happened or they are somewhere bad.

from "A LITTLE PRINCESS" - Part II

by Frances Hodgson Burnett

During her short life only one thing had troubled her, and that thing was "the place" she was to be taken to some day. The climate of India was very bad for children. As soon as possible they were sent away from it—generally to England and to school. She had seen other children go away. She had heard their fathers and mothers talk about the letters they received from them. She had known that she would be obliged to go also. Though sometimes her father's stories of the voyage and the new country had attracted her, she had been troubled by the thought that he could not stay with her.

"Couldn't you go to that place with me, papa?" she had asked when she was five years old. "Couldn't you go to school, too? I would help you with your lessons."

"But you will not have to stay for a very long time, little Sara," he had always said. "You will go to a nice house where there will be a lot of little girls. You will play together. I will send you plenty of books. You will grow so fast that it will seem scarcely a year before you are big enough and clever enough to come back and take care of papa."

She had liked to think of that. To keep the house for her father; to ride with him, and sit at the head of his table when he had dinner parties; to talk to him and read his books—that would be what she would like most in the world, and if one must go away to "the place" in England to attain it, she must make up her mind to go. She did not care very much for other little girls, but if she had plenty of books she could console herself. She liked books more than anything else. She was, in fact, always inventing stories of beautiful things and telling them to herself. Sometimes she had told them to her father. He had liked them as much as she did.

"Well, papa," she said softly, "if we are here I suppose we must be resigned."

He laughed at her old-fashioned speech and kissed her. He was really not at all resigned himself, though he knew he must keep that a secret. His quaint little Sara had been a great companion to him. He felt he should be a lonely fellow when, on his return to India, he went into his bungalow knowing he need not expect to see the small figure in its white frock come forward to meet him. So he held her very closely in his arms as the cab rolled into the big, dull square in which stood the house which was their destination.

1. Read the sentence below from the story.

She did not care very much for other little girls, but if she had plenty of books she could <u>console</u> herself.

In the sentence, the word <u>console</u> probably means

A. read.
(B.) comfort.
C. think about.
D. talk to.

2. According to the story, where is Sarah **probably** going?

(A) a boarding school
B. a summer camp
C. a new orphanage
D. a relative's house

3. What was it about the idea of going to "the place" that troubled Sara the **most**? Use details from the story to support your answer.

Sara wouldn't be able to be at School with her dad so she'll be alone.

TWO POEMS

by Paul Laurence Dunbar

Paul Laurence Dunbar was the first African American to gain national fame as a poet. He was born in 1872 in Dayton, Ohio to ex-slaves. He attended school with Orville Wright, one of the Wright brothers.

Dunbar was a prolific writer. He wrote short stories, novels, plays, songs and essays. He became most well-known for his poetry. He was popular with black and white readers of his day. His works are celebrated today by scholars and schoolchildren alike.

His style encompasses two distinct voices: the standard English of the classical poet, and the dialect of the turn-of-the-century black community in America. In poetry, he was gifted in using dialect to convey character. Paul Laurence Dunbar was only 33 years old when he died.

"AN EASY-GOIN' FELLER"

Ther' ain't no use in all this strife,
An' hurryin', pell-mell, right thro' life.
I don't believe in goin' too fast
To see what kind o' road you've passed.
ain't no mortal kind o' good,
'N' I wouldn't hurry ef I could.
I like to jest go joggin' 'long,
To limber up my soul with song;
To stop awhile 'n' chat the men,
'N' drink some cider now an' then.

Don' want no boss a-standin' by
To see me work; I allus try
To do my dooty right straight up,
An' earn what fills my plate an' cup.
An' ez fur boss, I'll be my own,
I like to jest be let alone,
To plough my strip an' tend my bees,
An' do jest like I doggoned please.
My head 's all right, an' my heart 's meller,
But I'm a easy-goin' feller.

"THE COLORED SOLDIERS"

If the muse were mine to tempt it
And my feeble voice were strong,
If my tongue were trained to measures,
I would sing a stirring song.
I would sing a song heroic
Of those noble sons of Ham,
Of the gallant colored soldiers
Who fought for Uncle Sam!

In the early days you scorned them,
And with many a flip and flout
Said "These battles are the white man's,
And the whites will fight them out."
Up the hills you fought and faltered,
In the vales you strove and bled,
While your ears still heard the thunder
Of the foes' advancing tread.

Then distress fell on the nation,
And the flag was drooping low;
Should the dust pollute your banner?
No! the nation shouted, No!
So when War, in savage triumph,
Spread abroad his funeral pall—
Then you called the colored soldiers,
And they answered to your call.

And like hounds unleashed and eager
For the life blood of the prey,
Sprung they forth and bore them bravely
In the thickest of the fray.
And where'er the fight was hottest,
Where the bullets fastest fell,
There they pressed unblanched and fearless
At the very mouth of hell.

Ah, they rallied to the standard
To uphold it by their might;
None were stronger in the labors,
None were braver in the fight.
From the blazing breach of Wagner
To the plains of Olustee,
They were foremost in the fight
Of the battles of the free.

And at Pillow! God have mercy
On the deeds committed there,
And the souls of those poor victims
Sent to Thee without a prayer.
Let the fullness of Thy pity
O'er the hot wrought spirits sway
Of the gallant colored soldiers
Who fell fighting on that day!

Yes, the Blacks enjoy their freedom,
And they won it dearly, too;
For the life blood of their thousands
Did the southern fields bedew.
In the darkness of their bondage,
In the depths of slavery's night,
Their muskets flashed the dawning,
And they fought their way to light.

They were comrades then and brothers,
Are they more or less to-day?
They were good to stop a bullet
And to front the fearful fray.
They were citizens and soldiers,
When rebellion raised its head;
And the traits that made them worthy—
Ah! those virtues are not dead.

They have shared your nightly vigils,
They have shared your daily toil;
And their blood with yours commingling
Has enriched the Southern soil.
They have met as fierce a foeman,
And have been as brave and true.

And their deeds shall find a record
In the registry of Fame;
For their blood has cleansed completely
Every blot of Slavery's shame.
So all honor and all glory
To those noble sons of Ham—
The gallant colored soldiers
Who fought for Uncle Sam!

1. Read the sentence below from the passage.

   Dunbar was a <u>prolific</u> writer. He wrote short stories, novels, plays, songs, and essays.

   In the sentence, the word <u>prolific</u> probably means

   A. producing much.
   B. knowledgeable about.
   C. entertaining well.
   D. pleasant enough.

2. Why weren't the colored soldiers asked to fight in the early days of the war?

   A. They were not needed.
   B. They were not liked.
   C. They were not free.
   D. They were not strong.

3. How does the speaker of the second poem **probably** feel about the colored soldiers?

   A. He thinks that they were kind.
   B. He thinks that they were brave.
   C. He thinks that they were misunderstood.
   D. He thinks that they were unimportant.

4. Which of these is the **best** summary of the poem?

   A. The black men did not want to fight in the white man's war, but they did want to win their freedom.
   B. The white soldiers were eager to fight alongside the black men, and were then bitter when they realized what good soldiers they turned out to be.
   C. The black men were excited to fight in the war, but became angry when they realized that they had been left out.
   D. The white soldiers overlooked the black men, and then enlisted them to fight at the forefront of the battle.

5. Which word **best** describes the speaker of the second poem?

   A. serious
   B. anxious
   C. funny
   D. proud

6. Compare the language and the tone of the two poems. Use details from the poems in to support your answer.

7. Do you think that the narrator of the first poem also might have been one of the heroes of the second poem? Explain why you do or do not think so. Use details from the poems in to support your answer.

from "THE INVISIBLE MAN"

by H.G. Wells

Exhausted and wounded as the Invisible Man was, he refused to accept Kemp's word that his freedom should be respected. He examined the two windows of the bedroom, drew up the blinds and opened the sashes, to confirm Kemp's statement that a retreat by them would be possible. Outside the night was very quiet and still, and the new moon was setting over the down. Then he examined the keys of the bedroom and the two dressing-room doors, to satisfy himself that these also could be made an assurance of freedom. Finally he expressed himself satisfied. He stood on the hearth-rug and Kemp heard the sound of a yawn.

"I'm sorry," said the Invisible Man, "if I cannot tell you all that I have done to-night. But I am worn out. It's grotesque, no doubt. It's horrible! But believe me, Kemp, in spite of your arguments of this morning, it is quit a possible thing. I have made a discovery. I meant to keep it to myself. I can't. I must have a partner. And you . . . We can do such things . . . But to-morrow. Now, Kemp, I feel as though I must sleep or perish."

Kemp stood in the middle of the room staring at the headless garment. "I suppose I must leave you," he said. "It's—incredible. Three things happening like this, overturning all my preconceptions—would make me insane. But it's real! Is there anything more that I can get you?"

"Only bid me good-night," said Griffin.

"Good-night," said Kemp, and shook an invisible hand. He walked sideways to the door. Suddenly the dressing-gown walked quickly towards him. "Understand me!" said the dressing-gown. "No attempts to hamper me, or capture me! Or—"

Kemp's face changed a little. "I thought I gave you my word," he said.

Kemp closed the door softly behind him, and the key was turned upon him forthwith. Then, as he stood with an expression of passive amazement on his face, the rapid feet came to the door of the dressing-room and that too was locked. Kemp slapped his brow with his hand. "Am I dreaming? Has the world gone mad—or have I?"

He laughed, and put his hand to the locked door. "Barred out of my own bedroom, by a flagrant absurdity!" he said.

He walked to the head of the staircase, turned, and stared at the locked doors. "It's fact," he said. He put his fingers to his slightly bruised neck. "Undeniable fact!

"But—"

He shook his head hopelessly, turned, and went downstairs.

1. Why did the Invisible Man **probably** examine the windows in the bedroom and the keys to the doors?

   A. He wanted to capture Kemp.
   B. He was planning an escape.
   C. He wanted to lock Kemp out.
   D. He was interested in houses.

2. Why did the Invisible Man want Kemp to leave?

   A. He was suspicious of Kemp.
   B. He was very tired.
   C. He was angry with Kemp.
   D. He needed a partner.

3. What was Griffin's reaction to becoming invisible? Use details from the story to support your answer.

from "A FANCY OF HERS"

by Horatio Alger

The stage rumbled along the main street of Granville. It drew up in front of the only hotel of which the village could boast. The driver descended from his throne. Coming round to the side he opened the door and addressed the only passenger remaining within.

"Where do you want to go, miss?"

A girl's face looked out inquiringly.

"Is this the hotel?" she asked.

"Yes, miss."

"I will get out here," she said quietly.

There were a few loungers on the piazza, which extended along the whole front of the building. As she descended with a light and springy step, disregarding the proffered aid of the driver, they eyed her curiously.

"Who is she, Abner?" Timothy Varnum asked the driver, as the stranger entered the house.

"I reckon she's the new school teacher," said Abner; "I heard Squire Hadley say she was expected today."

"Where does she come from?"

"York State, somewhere. I don't justly know where."

"Looks like a city gal."

"Mebbe, though I don't think it would pay a city gal to come to Granville to teach."

Unconscious of the curiosity which her appearance had excited, the girl entered the open entry and paused. A middle-aged woman, evidently the landlady of the inn, speedily made her appearance.

"Good afternoon, miss," she said. "Shall I show you to a room?"

"Thank you," said the stranger, gratefully. "I shall be very glad if you will. The ride has been warm and dusty. My trunks are on the stage—"

"All right, miss, I'll have them sent up. If you'll follow me upstairs, I'll give you a room." She led the way into a front room, very plainly furnished, but with a pleasant view of the village from the windows.

"I think you will find everything you require," she said, preparing to go. "Supper will be ready in half an hour, but you can have it later if you wish."

"I shall be ready, thank you."

Left alone, the stranger sank into a wooden rocking chair, and gazed thoughtfully from the window.

"Well, I have taken the decisive step," she said to herself. "It may be a mad freak, but I must not draw back now. Instead of going to Newport or to Europe, I have deliberately agreed to teach the grammar school in this out of the way country place. I am wholly unknown here, and it is hardly likely that any of my friends will find me out. For the first time in my life I shall make myself useful—perhaps. Or will my experiment end in failure? That is a question which time alone can solve."

1. How did the people react when the girl **first** walked into the hotel?

   A. shocked
   B. confused
   C. curious
   D. upset

2. Read the sentence below from the story.

   "Well, I have taken the <u>decisive</u> step."

   In the sentence, the word <u>decisive</u> probably means

   A. scary.
   B. common.
   C. new.
   D. momentous.

3. What is the girl's "experiment?" Why would some people think it is a "mad freak?" Use details from the story to support your answer.

AMELIA EARHART

Amelia Earhart was born in Atchison, Kansas, on July 24, 1897. In those days, airplanes were not nearly as common as they are today. Earhart was 12 years old before she ever saw an airplane. She did not take her first flight until 1920. Amelia Earhart was so thrilled by her first airplane ride that she quickly began to take flying lessons. She wrote, "As soon as I left the ground, I knew I myself had to fly."

Earhart excelled as a pilot. Her first instructor was Neta Snook. Snook was one of the first women to graduate from the Curtiss School of Aviation. Earhart borrowed money from her mother to buy a two-seat plane. She got her U.S. flying license in December 1921. By October 1922, she had set an altitude record for women of 14,000 feet. In 1923, Earhart received her international pilot's license. She was only the sixteenth woman to do so.

In 1928, Amelia Earhart received a phone call that would change her life. She was invited to become the first woman passenger to cross the Atlantic Ocean in a plane. "The idea of just going as 'extra weight' did not appeal to me at all," she said. She accepted the offer nonetheless. On June 17, 1928, Amelia Earhart flew in a plane named *Friendship* with copilots Wilmer "Bill" Stultz and Louis "Slim" Gordon. The plane landed at Burry Port, South Wales. It had just a small amount of fuel left. Earhart's first trip across the Atlantic had taken more than twenty hours!

After that flight, Earhart became a media sensation. Following the trip, she was given parties and even a ticker-tape parade down Broadway in New York City. President Coolidge called to congratulate her on crossing the Atlantic. Because Earhart's record-breaking career and physical appearance were similar to pioneering pilot and American hero Charles Lindbergh, she earned the nickname "Lady Lindy."

After flying across the Atlantic as a passenger in 1928, Amelia Earhart's next goal was to achieve a transatlantic crossing alone. In 1927, Charles Lindbergh became the first person to make a solo nonstop flight across the Atlantic. In 1932, exactly five years after Lindbergh's flight, Earhart became the first woman to repeat the feat. Her popularity grew even more. She was the undisputed queen of the air! Still, she wanted to achieve more. She decided that her next trip would be to fly around the world.

In June 1937, she began a flight around the world with Fred Noonan as her navigator. No one knows why, but she left behind important communication and navigation instruments. Perhaps it was to make room for additional fuel for the long flight. The pair made it to New Guinea in 21 days, even though Earhart was tired and ill. During the next leg of the trip, they departed New Guinea for Howland Island, a tiny island in the middle of the Pacific Ocean. July 2, 1937, was the last time that Earhart and Noonan communicated with a nearby Coast Guard ship. They were never heard from again.

The U.S. Navy conducted a massive search for Earhart and Noonan that continued for more than two weeks. Some admirers were unable to accept that Earhart had simply disappeared. They believed that she had been captured by enemies of the United States. Neither the plane nor Earhart nor Noonan were ever found. No one knows for sure what happened. Many people believe that they got lost and simply ran out of fuel, crashed, and died. At the time, Amelia Earhart was less than a month away from her fortieth birthday.

1. What record did Amelia Earhart set in 1922?

   A. She flew higher than any woman had ever flown.
   B. She flew further than any woman had ever flown.
   C. She flew longer than any woman had ever flown.
   D. She flew faster than any woman had ever flown.

2. Amelia Earhart **first** became famous for flying

   A. by herself across the Atlantic Ocean.
   B. as a passenger across the Atlantic.
   C. solo around the world in 80 days.
   D. by herself across the United States.

3. Which sentence **best** summarizes the passage?

   A. Early in life, Amelia Earhart decided that she wanted to fly, and she became a well-known American because of her flying adventures.
   B. Amelia Earhart was an inexperienced pilot who disappeared in 1937 shortly after she began her first plane flight.
   C. Charles Lindbergh, who was a well-known pilot, inspired Amelia Earhart and she later became known as "Lady Lindy."
   D. Amelia Earhart learned from the U.S. Navy how to fly and she led the first American flight across the Atlantic Ocean.

4. Why do you think people believed that Amelia Earhart had been captured, not lost? Use details from the passage to support your answer.

She had most likly been captured because the us Navy was following her and the radio just cut and stoped.

from "THE VELVETEEN RABBIT"

by Margery Williams Bianco

THERE was once a velveteen rabbit. In the beginning he was really splendid. He was fat and bunchy, as a rabbit should be. His coat was spotted brown and white. He had real thread whiskers. His ears were lined with pink sateen. On Christmas morning, when he sat wedged in the top of the Boy's stocking, with a sprig of holly between his paws, the effect was charming.

There were other things in the stocking, nuts and oranges and a toy engine, and chocolate almonds and a clockwork mouse, but the Rabbit was quite the best of all. For at least two hours the Boy loved him. Then Aunts and Uncles came to dinner, and there was a great rustling of tissue paper and unwrapping of parcels, and in the excitement of looking at all the new presents the Velveteen Rabbit was forgotten.

For a long time he lived in the toy cupboard or on the nursery floor, and no one thought very much about him. He was naturally shy, and being only made of velveteen, some of the more expensive toys quite snubbed him. The mechanical toys were very superior, and looked down upon every one else; they were full of modern ideas, and pretended they were real. The model boat, who had lived through two seasons and lost most of his paint, caught the tone from them and never missed an opportunity of referring to his rigging in technical terms.

The Rabbit could not claim to be a model of anything, for he didn't know that real rabbits existed. He thought they were all stuffed with sawdust like him. He understood that sawdust was quite out-of-date and should never be mentioned in modern circles. Even Timothy, the jointed wooden lion, who was made by the disabled soldiers, and should have had broader views, put on airs and pretended he was connected with Government. Between them all the poor little Rabbit was made to feel himself very insignificant and commonplace. The only person who was kind to him at all was the Skin Horse.

The Skin Horse had lived longer in the nursery than any of the others. He was so old that his brown coat was bald in patches and showed the seams underneath. Most of the hairs in his tail had been pulled out to string bead necklaces. He was wise, for he had seen a long succession of mechanical toys arrive to boast and swagger, and by-and-by break their mainsprings and pass away. He knew that they were only toys, and would never turn into anything else. For nursery magic is very strange and wonderful, and only those playthings that are old and wise and experienced like the Skin Horse understand all about it.

"What is REAL?" asked the Rabbit one day, when they were lying side by side near the nursery fender, before Nana came to tidy the room. "Does it mean having things that buzz inside you and a stick-out handle?"

"Real isn't how you are made," said the Skin Horse. "It's a thing that happens to you. When a child loves you for a long, long time, not just to play with, but REALLY loves you, then you become Real."

"Does it hurt?" asked the Rabbit.

"Sometimes," said the Skin Horse, for he was always truthful. "When you are Real you don't mind being hurt."

"Does it happen all at once, like being wound up," he asked, "or bit by bit?"

"It doesn't happen all at once," said the Skin Horse. "You become. It takes a long time. That's why it doesn't happen often to people who break easily, or have sharp edges, or who have to be carefully kept. Generally, by the time you are Real, most of your hair has been loved off, and your eyes drop out and you get loose in your joints and very shabby. But these things don't matter at all, because once you are Real you can't be ugly, except to people who don't understand."

"I suppose you are real?" said the Rabbit. And then he wished he had not said it, for he thought the Skin Horse might be sensitive. But the Skin Horse only smiled.

"The Boy's Uncle made me Real," he said. "That was a great many years ago; but once you are Real you can't become unreal again. It lasts for always."

1. Read the sentence below from the story.

   Between them all the poor little Rabbit was made to feel himself very <u>insignificant</u> and commonplace.

   In the sentence, the word <u>insignificant</u> probably means

   A. moving parts.
   B. soft and silky.
   C. not important.
   D. extra-special.

2. Which was the **most** self-important toy?

   A. a model boat
   B. a mechanical toy
   C. the wooden lion
   D. the Skin Horse

3. Which was the wisest toy?

A. the model boat
B. a mechanical toy
C. the wooden lion
D. the Skin Horse

4. According to the Skin Horse, what made a toy "Real"?

A. uncles
B. stick-out handles
C. bald spots
D. undying love

5. How was a toy **different** after it became "Real"? Use details from the story to support your answer.

In this story real would be basically A bond between the owner and the toy it dosen't really Microsc the idea that there real because they are made it really depends how insignifigant They are to a human. A Toy would be different by having a bond with some-one.

I mean haveing a bond with some-thing one. When I mean "bond" haveing a relationship so that basically you play or use the toy more usually than other

And how is it different? you may ask.
it can differ on the type they can
be more wise clever or be more foolish

CHICKEN FEATHERS

Walter Schmidt is a chemist with the Agricultural Research Service. You can bet that when he was a kid, he never told his Mom, "I'm going to study hard and go to college. I want to spend all day making boats out of chicken feathers and playing with them!" She probably would have made Walter clean up his room. Chemist Schmidt made the boat as a way of cleaning up the world. The boat, he explains, is just an easy example of what could be made by mixing fiberglass with a major agricultural leftover: chicken feathers.

Schmidt's job is to study the size, shape and chemical properties of all kinds of substances and materials. Doing this with chicken feathers has led Schmidt to find valuable new ways to recycle the feathers. Toy-boat building isn't really one of them, although canoes made of a fiberglass-chicken feather mixture are a possibility.

Why recycle chicken feathers? Each year, more than two billion pounds of feathers are produced by the U.S. poultry industry. That is enough to fill more than a billion pillowcases! Figuring out what to do with all those feathers can be a real headache! Most farmers throw them away, or they grind them up and mix them into animal feed to add protein to animal diets.

Schmidt, as an environmental chemist, is always looking for ways to benefit the environment, such as by keeping mountains of feathers out of landfills. Schmidt put a feather under a powerful electron microscope to get a close look at each piece or "barb" of a feather on a quill. What others see as feather, Schmidt sees as "keratin" fiber.

Keratin is the same type of fiber as those found in wool. It gives wool clothes the ability to stay dry even in the rain. The keratin fibers in feathers are shorter and finer than those in wool, but just as strong.

Keratin fibers in chicken feathers are much stronger and more absorbent than wood fibers—called "plant cellulose." Keratin also breaks down in landfills much faster than plastic. Besides the model boat, Schmidt has tinkered with chicken-feather fibers to make other things. Just a few of the things Schmidt has made are dyed paper, cloth, paper plant pots, and air filters for buildings and cars.

Speaking of cars, Schmidt has also blended feathers and plastic to make materials that could be molded into auto dashboards and door panels. Do you think, though, that a car named the "Cluckmobile" would be a big seller? They may need to work on the name.

"Insulation for homes is another possibility," says Schmidt. And, he has gone to different companies to see if they could use their machines to make new test products out of chicken feathers. So far, they've made diapers and filters as well as insulation.

Schmidt says that the feather fibers can come from any bird. However, commercial chickens have built-in color control: they're bred to always have the same white feathers.

1. According to the passage, what is one use for feather fibers?

A. paper
B. wood
C. ink
D. fiberglass

2. What breaks down faster than plastic in a landfill?

A. fiberglass canoes
B. keratin fiber
C. auto dashboards
D. plant cellulose

3. Why are chicken feathers better to use than feathers from other birds? Use details from the passage to support your answer.

They have more keraitn than other fedther from other birds

"ODIN & THOR"

from Bulfinch's Mythology: The Age of Fable

Valhalla is the great hall of Odin, wherein he feasts with his chosen heroes, all those who have fallen bravely in battle, for all who die a peaceful death are excluded. The flesh of the boar Schrimnir is served up to them, and is abundant for all. For although this boar is cooked every morning, he becomes whole again every night. For drink the heroes are supplied abundantly with mead from the she-goat Heidrum. When the heroes are not feasting they amuse themselves with fighting. Every day they ride out into the court or field and fight until they cut each other in pieces. This is their pastime; but when mealtime comes they recover from their wounds and return to feast in Valhalla. From Odin's name, spelled "W-o-d-e-n," as it sometimes is, came "Wednesday," the name of the fourth day of the week.

Thor, the "thunderer," Odin's eldest son, is the strongest of gods and men, and possesses three very precious things. The first is a hammer, which both the Frost and the Mountain giants know to their cost, when they see it hurled against them in the air, for it has split many a skull of their fathers and kindred. When thrown, it returns to his hand of its own accord. The second rare thing he possesses is called the belt of strength. When he girds it about him his divine might is doubled. The third, also very precious, is his iron gloves, which he puts on whenever he would use his mallet efficiently. From Thor's name is derived our word "Thursday."

1. Which **best** summarizes the story?

   A. Schrimnir the boar was eaten every day and grew again every night.
   B. The residents of Valhalla held great feasts and fought one another daily.
   C. The mighty gods Odin and Thor were remembered on the modern calendar.
   D. Odin's son Thor defeated the fathers and families of the Mountain giants.

2. In the second paragraph, the word <u>accord</u> probably means

   A. disturbance.
   B. decision.
   C. enormity.
   D. explorations.

3. With whom did Odin feast?

A. all soldiers
B. chosen heroes
C. hidden enemies
D. peaceful soldiers

4. Which English word is derived from Thor's name?

A. Thomas
B. thunder
C. Thursday
D. thrown

5. Where do you think the names "Sunday" and "Monday" come from? Do all cultures use the same names for days? Use details from the story to support your answer.

For Sunday I think it came from "Satwon" witch is a Roman god and for Monday it's meracury also one

[redacted]

from "BURNING DAYLIGHT"

by Jack London

Few men knew Elam Harnish by any other name than "Burning Daylight," the name which had been given him in the early days in the land because of his habit of routing his comrades out of their blankets with the complaint that daylight was burning. Of the pioneers in that far Arctic wilderness, where all men were pioneers, he was reckoned among the oldest. Men like Al Mayo and Jack McQuestion antedated him; but they had entered the land by crossing the Rockies from the Hudson Bay country to the east. He, however, had been the pioneer over the Chilcoot and Chilcat passes. In the spring of 1883, twelve years before, a stripling of eighteen, he had crossed over the Chilcoot with five comrades.

In the fall he had crossed back with one. Four had perished by mischance in the bleak, uncharted vastness. And for twelve years Elam Harnish had continued to grope for gold among the shadows of the Circle.

And no man had groped so obstinately nor so enduringly. He had grown up with the land. He knew no other land. Civilization was a dream of some previous life. Camps like Forty Mile and Circle City were to him metropolises. And not alone had he grown up with the land, for, raw as it was, he had helped to make it. He had made history and geography, and those that followed wrote of his traverses and charted the trails his feet had broken.

Heroes are seldom given to hero-worship, but among those of that young land, young as he was, he was accounted an elder hero. In point of time he was before them. In point of deed he was beyond them. In point of endurance it was acknowledged that he could kill the hardiest of them. Furthermore, he was accounted a nervy man, a square man, and a white man.

In all lands where life is a hazard lightly played with and lightly flung aside, men turn, almost automatically, to gambling for diversion and relaxation. In the Yukon men gambled their lives for gold, and those that won gold from the ground gambled for it with one another. Nor was Elam Harnish an exception. He was a man's man primarily, and the instinct in him to play the game of life was strong. Environment had determined what form that game should take. He was born on an Iowa farm, and his father had emigrated to eastern Oregon, in which mining country Elam's boyhood was lived. He had known nothing but hard knocks for big stakes. Pluck and endurance counted in the game, but the great god Chance dealt the cards. Honest work for sure but meager returns did not count. A man played big. He risked everything for everything, and anything less than everything meant that he was a loser.

So for twelve Yukon years, Elam Harnish had been a loser. True, on Moosehide Creek the past summer he had taken out twenty thousand dollars, and what was left in the ground was twenty thousand more. But, as he himself proclaimed, that was no more than getting his ante back. He had ante'd his life for a dozen years, and forty thousand was a small pot for such a stake—the price of a drink and a dance at the Tivoli, of a winter's flutter at Circle City, and a grubstake for the year to come.

1. What will **probably** happen next?

   A. Harnish will lose all his money gambling.
   B. Harnish will continue searching for gold.
   C. The gold hunters will leave the Yukon.
   D. Civilization will finally reach the Yukon.

2. Read the sentence below from the passage.

   In all lands where life is a <u>hazard</u> lightly played with and lightly flung aside, men turn, almost automatically, to gambling for diversion and relaxation.

   In the sentence, the word <u>hazard</u> probably means

   A. a risk.
   B. something unimportant.
   C. comprehension.
   D. safety.

3. The author describes Elam Harnish as a loser in order to show that he had

   A. found more gold than most others.
   B. failed at becoming wealthy.
   C. not learned how to play cards games very well.
   D. had failed at learning how to survive in the wild.

4. Harnish **probably** lives in the wilderness because

   A. he is farming new land.
   B. he is looking for new cities.
   C. he is searching for gold.
   D. he is meeting new people.

5. What is the **most** likely reason Harnish takes so many chances?

   A. He has had a tough childhood in a mining community.
   B. He wants to be known as a hero.
   C. He works on a farm throughout his entire life.
   D. He knows that one day he will settle down and stop traveling.

6. Do you agree with the author's statement that Harnish was "a loser"? Why or why not? Use details from the story to support your answer.

No, because Harnish is not the only setteler tring to find gold, but however they fail to sucsess to find the gold.

So in my opinion Harnish is Not a "Loser". He also Placed a great amount of perserverance to come to North america in the search of gold. Even worse he went to the Yukon witch is a freezing territory.

from "THE MASTER THIEF" - Part I

by Andrew Lang

The Governor of the province had such a large house and so much money that he did not even know how much it was. He had a daughter too who was both pretty and dainty, and good and wise. The Master Thief was determined to have her as his wife. He told his father that he was to go to the Governor, and ask for his daughter for him. "If he asks what trade I follow, you may say that I am a Master Thief," said he.

"I think you must be crazy," said the man, "for you can't be in your senses if you think of anything so foolish."

"You must go to the Governor and beg for his daughter—there is no help," said the youth.

So [the father] told [the Governor] that he had three sons who had gone away one day, and how he had given them permission to go where they chose, and take to whatsoever work they fancied. "Now," he said, "the youngest of them has come home, and . . . I have come to you to ask for your daughter for him, and I am to say that he is a Master Thief."

"Console yourself, my man," said the Governor, laughing. "You may tell him from me that he must first give me some proof of this. If he can steal the joint off the spit in the kitchen on Sunday, when every one of us is watching it, he shall have my daughter. Will you tell him that?"

The man did tell him, and the youth thought it would be easy enough to do it. So he set himself to work to catch three hares alive, put them in a bag, clad himself in some old rags so that he looked so poor and wretched that it was quite pitiable to see him, and in this guise on Sunday forenoon he sneaked into the passage with his bag, like any beggar boy. The Governor himself and everyone in the house was in the kitchen, keeping watch over the joint. While they were doing this the youth let one of the hares slip out of his bag, and off it set and began to run round the yard.

"Just look at that hare," said the people in the kitchen, and wanted to go out and catch it.

The Governor saw it too, but said, "Oh, let it go! It's no use to think of catching a hare when it's running away."

It was not long before the youth let another hare out, and the people in the kitchen saw this too, and thought that it was the same. So again they wanted to go out and catch it, but the Governor again told them that it was of no use to try.

Very soon afterwards, however, the youth let slip the third hare, and it set off and ran round and round the courtyard. The people in the kitchen saw this too, and believed that it was still the same hare that was running about, so they wanted to go out and catch it.

"It's a remarkably fine hare!" said the Governor. "Come and let us see if we can get hold of it." So out he went, and the others with him, and away went the hare, and they after it, in real earnest.

In the meantime, however, the Master Thief took the joint and ran off with it, and whether the Governor got any roast meat for his dinner that day I know not, but I know that he had no roast hare, though he chased it till he was both hot and tired . . .

1. The story is **mainly** about

   A. the Master Thief deciding to trick the Governor and marry his daughter.
   B. a father needing to explain to the Governor why his son is a Master Thief.
   C. dinner guests seeing three hares in the yard and wanting to go out to chase them.
   D. the Master Thief dressing in ragged clothing and catching three hares.

2. What happened after the Master Thief released the third hare?

   A. He said he should meet the Governor's daughter.
   B. The Governor joined people chasing the hare.
   C. The Governor visited the kitchen to see the joint.
   D. He stole the joint from the kitchen and ran off.

3. How does the Master Thief feel about the Governor's challenge?

   A. excited
   B. frightened
   C. confident
   D. nervous

4. What caused the man to go to the Governor?

   A. His son wanted to hunt in the Governor's yard for hare.
   B. He decided to steal the Governor's daughter to show that he was a thief.
   C. He wanted the Governor's help in finding the three sons who left him.
   D. His son sent him to ask permission to marry the Governor's daughter.

5. Read the sentence below from the passage.

   So he set himself to work to catch three hares alive, put them in a bag, clad himself in some old rags so that he looked so poor and wretched that it was quite pitiable to see him, and in this guise on Sunday forenoon he sneaked into the passage with his bag, like any beggar boy.

   In the sentence, the word pitiable probably means

   A. sad.
   B. clever.
   C. tricky.
   D. difficult.

from "THE MASTER THIEF" - Part II

by Andrew Lang

The Master Thief came and wanted to have the Governor's daughter according to the Governor's promise. The Governor once more gave him nothing but fine words, and said, "You must give me one more proof of your skill, so that I can really judge of your worth. I have twelve horses in my stable. I will put twelve stable boys in the stable, one on each horse. If you are clever enough to steal the horses from under them, I will see what I can do for you."

"What you set me to do can be done," said the Master Thief, "but am I certain to get your daughter when it is done?"

"Yes; if you can do that, I will do my best for you," said the Governor.

So the Master Thief went to a shop, and bought enough brandy to fill two pocket flasks. He put a sleeping drink into one of these flasks, but into the other he poured brandy only. Then he engaged eleven men to lie that night in hiding behind the Governor's stable.

After this, by fair words and good payment, he borrowed a ragged gown and a jerkin from an aged woman. Then, with a staff in his hand and a poke on his back, he hobbled off as evening came on towards the Governor's stable. The stable boys were just watering the horses for the night, and it was quite as much as they could do to attend to that.

"What on earth do you want here?" said one of them to the old woman.

"Oh dear! oh dear! How cold it is!" she said, sobbing, and shivering with cold.

"Oh dear! oh dear! It's cold enough to freeze a poor old body to death!" and she shivered and shook again, and said, "For heaven's sake give me leave to stay here and sit just inside the stable door."

"You will get nothing of the kind! Be off this moment! If the Governor were to catch sight of you here, he would lead us a pretty dance," said one.

"Oh! what a poor helpless old creature!" said another, who felt sorry for her. "That poor old woman can do no harm to anyone. She may sit there and welcome."

The rest of them thought that she ought not to stay, but while they were disputing about this and looking after the horses, she crept farther and farther into the stable, and at last sat down behind the door, and when once she was inside no one took any more notice of her.

As the night wore on the stable boys found it rather cold work to sit still on horseback.

"Hutetu! But it is fearfully cold!" said one, and began to beat his arms backwards and forwards across his breast.

"Yes, I am so cold that my teeth are chattering," said another.

"If one had but a little tobacco," said a third.

Well, one of them had a little, so they shared it among them, though there was very little for each man, but they chewed it. This was some help to them, but very soon they were just as cold as before.

"Hutetu!" said one of them, shivering again.

"Hutetu!" said the old woman, gnashing her teeth together till they chattered inside her mouth. Then she got out the flask which contained nothing but brandy, and her hands trembled so that she shook the bottle about, and when she drank it made a great gulp in her throat.

"What is that you have in your flask, old woman?" asked one of the stable boys.

"Oh, it's only a little drop of brandy, your honour," she said.

"Brandy! What! Let me have a drop! Let me have a drop!" screamed all the twelve at once.

"Oh, but what I have is so little," whimpered the old woman. "It will not even wet your mouths."

But they were determined to have it, and there was nothing to be done but give it; so she took out the flask with the sleeping drink and put it to the lips of the first of them; and now she shook no more, but guided the flask so that each of them got just as much as he ought, and the twelfth had not done drinking before the first was already sitting snoring. Then the Master Thief flung off his beggar's rags, and took one stable boy after the other and gently set him astride on the partitions which divided the stalls, and then he called his eleven men who were waiting outside, and they rode off with the Governor's horses.

In the morning when the Governor came to look after his stable boys they were just beginning to come to again. They were driving their spurs into the partition till the splinters flew about, and some of the boys fell off, and some still hung on and sat looking like fools.

"Ah, well," said the Governor, "it is easy to see who has been here; but what a worthless set of fellows you must be to sit here and let the Master Thief steal the horses from under you!" And they all got a beating for not having kept watch better.

1. Why does the Master Thief dress up as an old woman?

A. to trick the stable boys
B. to confuse the Governor
C. to hide from the police
D. to get pity from others

2. The author repeats the word "Hutetu" in order to

A. make the action of the story seem more exciting.
B. let the reader know that the plan was dangerous.
C. emphasize to the reader how cold it was outside.
D. show how the Master Thief feels about the Governor.

3. Which word **best** describes how the stable boys feel at the end of the story?

A. frightened
B. foolish
C. positive
D. astounded

4. What do you think will **probably** happen next?

A. The thief will return the joint to the kitchen spit.
B. The Governor and the thief's father will marry.
C. The thief will release a fourth hare into the yard.
D. The Governor will challenge the thief again.

5. What does the old woman want from the stable boys?

A. food
B. water
C. shelter
D. friendship

6. Which of the following describes the Master Thief's **major** conflict?

A. The Governor wants to have the Master Thief put behind bars.
B. The Governor wants the Master Thief to steal from an old lady.
C. The Governor will not let the Master Thief take back his horses.
D. The Governor will not let the Master Thief marry his daughter.

8. What kind of person do you think the Master Thief is? Use details from the story to support your answer.

He is determand to marry the governor's daugter so he went to ask. As he asked the governor gave him challenges if he sacceeds he can have the govenor's daugter. However the governor keeps trowing challanges At the Master theif.

Looking at the story it Apeels that the Master theif is going to do any thing to marry the govenor's daugter.

Or Looking back the govenor dosen't want Master theif to marry his daugter. That could be a reason ~~that~~ they are not married yet.

Master Theif also could have a sneackey plan up his sleaves so The govonor might have a suspicion on Master theif. A suspicion might be he would corupt or he might steel the govenor's wealth.

That explaing how sneaky he is he can dress or act like someone else And not knowing thet it's him. That's why he's Master theif.

As a result his personality is mystrious. in the passage not even his name is mencioned or cited.

A PREPARATOR

What creature sees like an artist, understands bones like a doctor, uses blowtorches and plastics like an engineer, and spends summers in the Gobi Desert? The answer is a preparator. Amy Davidson is a preparator for the American Museum of Natural History. She works in the Department of Vertebrate Paleontology in New York City.

As a youngster, Davidson did not dream of one day working with dinosaurs. She did, however, love the outdoors. She also loved to make sculptures. In college she studied art. Her first job was with the exhibition department of the Smithsonian Institution in Washington, D.C. There she built dioramas for the new Hall of Plant Evolution.

Amy Davidson left the Smithsonian to pursue sculpting. She worked at several jobs. She was an apprentice at a bronze foundry. There she learned to cast bronze sculptures. Later she worked for Harvard University's Department of Mammalogy. Her job was dissecting and preserving animals that had died. She also took classes in vertebrate paleontology and human anatomy.

Davidson's love of both art and science led her to a career turning point. A fossil preparator at Harvard invited her to work in his lab. Her first complete preparation revealed a perfect little creature under the microscope. It was curled up as if in sleep. It was a sleep of two hundred million years. She was hooked.

Davidson's most exciting adventure began later, when she came to work at the American Museum of Natural History. Ten days after starting as a preparator, she was on a plane with two paleontologists. They were heading halfway around the world. They were flying to Ulan Bator, Mongolia, on an expedition to the Gobi Desert.

The highlight of this 1993 expedition was the discovery of Oviraptor fossils. One Oviraptor was found protecting a nest of 22 eggs, possibly from a smothering dust storm that had swept the Gobi about 80 million years ago. An expedition in 1995 turned up two more Oviraptor skeletons found quite close together.

When the 1995 fossils arrived back in New York, Davidson went to work carefully cleaning and restoring one of the specimens. When she finished, the specimen was the most nearly perfect Oviraptor skeleton ever found.

"Working on a new fossil is like a window into the past," she says. "It's hard to go home at night. I want to stay and continue working, chipping away at the rock that encases the fossil. As I work, a natural sculpture, a skeleton, begins to emerge from the rock. So beautiful." So speaks an artist and a scientist.

1. The passage is **mainly** about

A. what you can learn a lot by studying history.
B. how art and science can work together.
C. how Amy Davidson found a job she loves.
D. why dinosaurs carefully protected their young.

2. In the eighth paragraph, the word <u>encases</u> probably means

A. saves.
B. removes.
C. packages.
D. becomes.

3. Amy Davidson learned to cast bronze sculptures when she worked

A. at the Smithsonian Institution.
B. at a foundry.
C. for Harvard University.
D. with dinosaur bones.

4. Describe what Amy Davidson does at work as a preparator. Use details from the passage to support your answer.

As a youngster she loved Sience and Arts, she would make sulptures. So when she got to colledge he studied art. So a little later she got a job at Smithsonian Institution as a Fist job.

A few years later, she worked at Harbords University department of mamalogy

She worked on Fosslibs and decided witch group it would go in and decided where the bones would go to create the full fossil.

from "THE DIAMOND AS BIG AS THE RITZ"

by F. Scott Fitzgerald

St. Midas' School is half an hour from Boston in a Rolls-Pierce motorcar. The actual distance will never be known, for no one, except John T. Unger, had ever arrived there save in a Rolls-Pierce and probably no one ever will again. St. Midas' is the most expensive and the most exclusive boys' preparatory school in the world.

John's first two years there passed pleasantly. The fathers of all the boys were money-kings and John spent his summers visiting at fashionable resorts. While he was very fond of all the boys he visited, their fathers struck him as being much of a piece, and in his boyish way he often wondered at their exceeding sameness.

When he told them where his home was they would ask jovially, "Pretty hot down there?" and John would muster a faint smile and answer, "It certainly is." His response would have been heartier had they not all made this joke—at best varying it with, "Is it hot enough for you down there?" which he hated just as much.

In the middle of his second year at school, a quiet, handsome boy named Percy Washington had been put in John's form. The newcomer was pleasant in his manner and exceedingly well dressed even for St. Midas', but for some reason he kept aloof from the other boys. The only person with whom he was intimate was John T. Unger, but even to John he was entirely uncommunicative concerning his home or his family. That he was wealthy went without saying, but beyond a few such deductions John knew little of his friend, so it promised rich confectionery for his curiosity when Percy invited him to spend the summer at his home "in the West." He accepted, without hesitation.

It was only when they were in the train that Percy became, for the first time, rather communicative. One day while they were eating lunch in the dining-car and discussing the imperfect characters of several of the boys at school, Percy suddenly changed his tone and made an abrupt remark.

"My father," he said, "is by far the richest man in the world."

"Oh," said John, politely. He could think of no answer to make to this confidence. He considered "That's very nice," but it sounded hollow and was on the point of saying, "Really?" but refrained since it would seem to question Percy's statement. And such an astounding statement could scarcely be questioned.

"By far the richest," repeated Percy.

"I was reading in the World Almanac," began John, "that there was one man in America with an income of over five million a year and four men with incomes of over three million a year, and—"

“Oh, they’re nothing.” Percy’s mouth was a half-moon of scorn. “Catchpenny capitalists, financial small-fry, petty merchants and money-lenders. My father could buy them out and not know he’d done it.”

“But how does he—”

“Why haven’t they put down *his* income tax? Because he doesn’t pay any. At least he pays a little one—but he doesn’t pay any on his *real* income.”

“He must be very rich,” said John simply. “I’m glad. I like very rich people.”

1. Read the sentence below from the passage

   St. Midas’ is the most expensive and the most <u>exclusive</u> boys’ preparatory school in the world.

   In the sentence, the word <u>exclusive</u> probably means

   A. beautiful.
   B. picky.
   C. difficult.
   D. interesting.

2. Which statement **best** describes how John feels about Percy?

   A. He is annoyed by Percy.
   B. He is frightened by Percy.
   C. He is worried about Percy.
   D. He is curious about Percy.

3. Why do the other boys’ fathers annoy John?

   A. They often insult his home.
   B. They all act the same way.
   C. They ask him about his father.
   D. They ask him to tell jokes.

4. What will **probably** happen next?

A. John and Percy will no longer be friends.
B. John and Percy won't return to school.
C. John will meet Percy's father.
(D.) John will decide to go home.

5. Where do you suppose John lives? Why do you think so? Use details from the story to support your answer.

Near boston or a few miles of st. Midas school Since in passadge "few miles off of St. Midas school" or another thing is "like 30 minutes".

We can infer that he lives 30 minuets away, But it also said in a "rolls-pierce car" so walking would be way more time to come or go.

So as a final decision he lives in boston.

The Opening Passage of "ALICE' S ADVENTURES IN WONDERLAND"

by Lewis Carroll

Alice was beginning to get very tired of sitting by her sister on the bank, and of having nothing to do: once or twice she had peeped into the book her sister was reading, but it had no pictures or conversations in it, "and what is the use of a book," thought Alice, "without pictures or conversations?"

So she was considering in her own mind (as well as she could, for the hot day made her feel very sleepy and stupid), whether the pleasure of making a daisy-chain would be worth the trouble of getting up and picking the daisies, when suddenly a White Rabbit with pink eyes ran close by her.

There was nothing so "very" remarkable in that; nor did Alice think it so "very" much out of the way to hear the Rabbit say to itself "Oh dear! Oh dear! I shall be too late!" (when she thought it over afterwards, it occurred to her that she ought to have wondered at this, but at the time it all seemed quite natural); but when the Rabbit actually *took a watch out of its waistcoat-pocket*, and looked at it, and then hurried on, Alice started to her feet, for it flashed across her mind that she had never before seen a rabbit with either a waistcoat-pocket, or a watch to take out of it, and, burning with curiosity, she ran across the field after it, and was just in time to see it pop down a large rabbit-hole under the hedge.

In another moment down went Alice after it, never once considering how in the world she was to get out again. The rabbit-hole went straight on like a tunnel for some way, and then dipped suddenly down, so suddenly that Alice had not a moment to think about stopping herself before she found herself falling down what seemed to be a very deep well. . . .

"Well!" thought Alice to herself. "After such a fall as this, I shall think nothing of tumbling down-stairs! How brave they'll all think me at home! Why, I wouldn't say anything about it, even if I fell off the top of the house!" (Which was very likely true.)

. . . "I wonder what Latitude or Longitude I've got to?" (Alice had not the slightest idea what Latitude was, or Longitude either, but she thought they were nice grand words to say.) . . .

Down, down, down. There was nothing to do, so Alice soon began talking again. "Dinah'll miss me very much to-night, I should think! . . . "

"I hope they'll remember her milk at teatime. Dinah, my dear! I wish you were down here with me! There are no mice in the air, I'm afraid, but you might catch a bat, and that's very like a mouse, you know . . . " And here Alice began to get rather sleepy . . . when suddenly, thump! thump! Down she came upon a heap of sticks and dry leaves, and the fall was over.

1. What is the **main** theme of this story?

   A. traveling underwater
   B. returning back home
   C. going to a playground
   D. having new experiences

2. Why isn't Alice interested in her sister's book?

   A. The book is too difficult for her to read.
   B. The book doesn't have any pictures.
   C. She has already read that book.
   D. She doesn't enjoy the book's plot.

3. What does Alice finally find "remarkable" about the rabbit?

   A. He has a watch.
   B. He runs very fast.
   C. He can talk.
   D. He can read.

4. Which word **best** describes how Alice feels as she is falling down the well?

   A. frightened
   B. surprised
   C. bored
   D. excited

5. What is the reason that Alice hopes someone will remember to give Dinah milk at teatime?

   A. Dinah puts milk in her tea.
   B. Dinah is Alice's little cat.
   C. Dinah is Alice's baby sister.
   D. Dinah likes cookies and milk.

6. The purpose of including the words "thump! thump!" is to

   A. let the readers know that Alice is out of danger.
   B. imitate the sound of Alice hitting the bottom.
   C. show the reader how Alice feels.
   D. give the story a more serious tone.

from "McTEAGUE: A STORY OF SAN FRANCISCO"

by Frank Norris

It was Sunday, and, according to his custom on that day, McTeague took his dinner at two in the afternoon at the car conductors' coffee-joint on Polk Street. He had a thick gray soup; heavy, underdone meat, very hot, on a cold plate; two kinds of vegetables; and a sort of suet pudding, full of strong butter and sugar. On his way back to his office, one block above, he stopped at Joe Frenna's saloon and bought a pitcher of steam beer. It was his habit to leave the pitcher there on his way to dinner.

Once in his office, or, as he called it on his signboard, "Dental Parlors," he took off his coat and shoes, unbuttoned his vest, and, having crammed his little stove full of coke, lay back in his operating chair at the bay window, reading the paper, drinking his beer, and smoking his huge porcelain pipe while his food digested; crop-full, stupid, and warm. By and by, gorged with steam beer, and overcome by the heat of the room, the cheap tobacco, and the effects of his heavy meal, he dropped off to sleep. Late in the afternoon his canary bird, in its gilt cage just over his head, began to sing. He woke slowly, finished the rest of his beer—very flat and stale by this time—and taking down his concertina from the bookcase, where in weekdays it kept the company of seven volumes of "Allen's Practical Dentist," played upon it some half-dozen very mournful airs.

McTeague looked forward to these Sunday afternoons as a period of relaxation and enjoyment. He invariably spent them in the same fashion. These were his only pleasures—to eat, to smoke, to sleep, and to play upon his concertina.

1. The story is **mainly** about a man

A. working on a Sunday afternoon.
B. relaxing at his office on a Sunday.
C. going out to lunch on a Sunday.
D. spending Sunday out with friends.

2. Which word **best** describes McTeague in this story?

A. reckless
B. scientific
C. merciless
D. leisurely

3. In the third paragraph, the word <u>fashion</u> probably means

A. clothes.
B. figure.
C. manner.
D. appearance.

CAR TIPS

When it comes to changing antifreeze, times have changed. It is no longer the rule to flush out the old and pour in the new every fall. Intervals for changing antifreeze have lengthened. Antifreeze formulations have improved. We now have upgraded metals in the cooling system as well.

Why replace antifreeze? Antifreeze contains corrosion inhibitors that wear out in time. Thanks to advances in antifreeze and cooling system technologies, some late-model cars don't need a change for four years. Some do not even need a change for five years. For most cars, however, changing the antifreeze every two years is recommended.

Another fluid needs constant attention, but not replacement. Windshield-washer fluid does not wear out. Always add fluid to keep the reservoir full. Some weather conditions use up a lot of washer fluid to maintain windshield visibility.

Car owners rarely think about the fuel filter until a problem develops. Trouble typically is signaled by loss of power when accelerating or going uphill. You may also notice difficulty in starting. Your car may be shaky while idling. The fuel filter has been doing its job by blocking particles of dirt and rust. It has become clogged. This reduces the flow of fuel.

Fuel filters should be replaced at intervals to avoid clogging. Owner's manuals vary in guidance. Some offer no specifics as to when to replace a filter. As a general rule, replace the filter annually or every thirty thousand miles at most.

Another serious problem for cars is a "knocking" engine. The noise that a driver will hear is a pinging or knocking sound. What this sound tells the driver is that detonation is taking place or could happen within a short period of time. Detonation, an explosion, occurs when the octane rating of the fuel isn't high enough to handle the heat and the pressure. When detonation happens, an engine is at risk for damage. Pressure and heat changes, which change the way the engine works, lead to the possibility of broken engine components. To prevent detonation from damaging your car, change to a higher level of octane for your fuel (check what the recommended level is for your car) and, as soon as you notice "knocking," take your car to a mechanic in order to prevent/check engine damage.

1. The author included the second paragraph in order to explain

A. when to replace a car's antifreeze.
B. why corrosion inhibitors wear out.
C. how antifreeze technology has advanced.
D. whether to mix water with antifreeze.

2. According to the passage, people should replace the antifreeze in their cars

A. every year.
B. every two years.
C. every four years.
D. every five years.

3. Some cars shake when they idle because of old

A. fuel.
B. washer fluid.
C. fuel filters.
D. antifreeze.

4. In the first paragraph, the word <u>intervals</u> probably means

A. difficult problems.
B. periods of time.
C. reasons.
D. guidelines.

5. Why does a car need antifreeze and windshield washer fluid? Use details from the passage to support your answer.

In a automobile, antifreeze and windshield water Fluid is a must. Adding to that, turning a blind Face to it is way it too ignorant. So, why do we need these factors? Your Car needs it as an organ, it helps it function. like without your eyes, you can't see. If a car does not have it's windshield water, every time you need to clean your car you got to step out and clean with water that can freeze or boil depending on the weather and might not even work.

THE WILDLIFE CONSERVATION SOCIETY

The Wildlife Conservation Society (WCS) has regional and thematic programs on four continents. Five of its programs are in New York City.

The Bronx Zoo, the first program, was founded in 1899. It has been a leader in wildlife conservation education since it opened. The Bronx Zoo is more than a zoo. It offers a variety of courses. The Bronx Zoo's Education Department also produces a full life-sciences curriculum. It is used in all 50 states. It is even used overseas.

The second program, the New York Aquarium is situated on 14 acres by the sea. It is in Coney Island, Brooklyn. It is home to thousands of fish and a multitude of marine creatures. These include beluga whales, sharks, walruses, and dolphins.

The third program invites you to discover the whole world of wildlife at the Central Park Wildlife Center. Trek through a tropical rain forest or cool down with the penguins, all in the middle of Manhattan.

Visit the Queens Wildlife Center in Flushing Meadows Park, the fourth program. You will experience an American wildlife adventure. You will see spectacled bears and come face to face with a mountain lion. You will stroll through the open aviary. Come discover majestic Roosevelt elk, American bison, and more.

The new Prospect Park Wildlife Center, the fifth program, invites children to use all their senses to discover an incredible world of wildlife. Tunnel through a prairie-dog town. Master the language of baboons. Create animal art, using meerkats as your models.

The Wildlife Conservation Society's programs extend to other regions of the world as well. In South America, WCS works extensively in Amazonian Brazil. It boasts one of the most extraordinary, yet least studied, ecosystems in the world. This ecosystem is the seasonally flooded forest known as the "varzea." In Asia, WCS works in the thick, wet forests just south of the extinct Crater Mountain Volcano in Papua, New Guinea. In Africa, the WCS works with all three gorilla subspecies: mountain gorillas, Grauer's gorillas, and western lowland gorillas.

1. The sixth paragraph is **mainly** about how

A. baboons have a secret language that humans don't know about.
B. the Prospect Park Center allows kids to experience wildlife.
C. kids can see a prairie dog town in the Prospect Park Center.
D. meerkats create their own art, as do many animals at the Center.

2. In the third paragraph, the word <u>multitude</u> probably means

A. structure.
B. dome.
C. percent.
D. mass.

3. What is one animal that visitors to the Central Park Wildlife Center might see?

A. a penguin
B. a gorilla
C. a mountain lion
D. a beluga whale

4. What is the author's **main** purpose for writing the passage?

A. to entertain readers with a story about endangered animals
B. to persuade readers to support their local animal shelters
C. to inform readers about a program that works to help animals
D. to explain to readers why it is dangerous to house exotic animals

5. Isn't it surprising that five wildlife centers are in New York City? Explain why it might make sense to put a wildlife center in the middle of a major city.

DOGS

The dog is considered to be the first domesticated animal. Dogs learned to live with people 14,000 years ago. There are many stories about how, in ancient times, man and wolves or wild dogs would share the same fire and even the same food, thereby learning long ago to become life-long companions.

Dogs can hear sounds more accurately than humans. Most people can't hear beyond a distance of 25 yards; dogs can hear sounds from as far away as 250 yards. A hot, dry nose does not necessarily indicate illness. Healthy dogs can have dry noses and many dogs with wet noses can be seriously ill. Change in behavior is the best indicator of disease.

Socialization is the process of exposing puppies to new sights, sounds, people, places and pets in a positive way. Socialized dogs are more comfortable with new environments, unfamiliar people, and other animals.

When deciding on which breed to buy, it is especially important that you consider what each dog is best suited for. For example, if you live in a small apartment in a major city, it is highly inadvisable to welcome a shepherding dog into your home. These dogs need to run free several times a day in wide-open spaces. A shepherding dog would most likely be extremely unhappy in a small, cramped apartment. Here are a few breeds you might consider, depending on where you live.

Toy and Small Breeds

Seniors and people who live in apartments or condos should look for lightweight, quiet dogs. They might look for dogs that are eager to please. The Cavalier King Charles Spaniel is a good choice, as is the Boston Terrier or Miniature Poodle. The Papillion is a happy, friendly dog. (It is named for the French word for "butterfly" because it has ears that resemble butterfly wings.) It is also suitable for small living spaces.

You might think that a small dog like the Jack Russell Terrier, a favorite for many people, would be a good apartment dog. However, this dog has a strong will, high energy, and strong hunting instincts. Learn about this breed before you consider adopting one. They need lots of attention and room to run and play several times throughout the day.

Working Breeds

Rottweiler puppies are irresistibly cute. It is important, though, to take care to discourage any behavior that would be undesirable in a 90-pound dog. In the future, that little puppy will be a big dog, a dog that will need to have a job to do or it will most likely find one for itself—and that could mean eating at least one of each of your shoes, if left lying around.

Working breeds were bred to instinctually like to take charge and take care of those they've learned to know as members of their "packs." Working dogs can typically easily be trained to become part of the police force, to help disabled people, or to guard a home or business. Other examples of working dogs are German Shepherds and Saint Bernards.

Hound Dog Breeds

Coonhounds exhibit loyalty and love toward their owners. Besides hunting, coonhounds participate in many other activities. These include agility trials, tracking, and search and rescue. The bloodhound is a breed with highly developed skills. It can follow a four-day-old track with its unique sense of smell.

Sheep Herding Breeds

Unlike hounds, which work mainly with their noses, sheep dogs use their sight and hearing more than their sense of smell. Some sheep-dog breeds include the Belgian Sheep Dog and the Border Collie. As mentioned, these dogs needs lots of room to run and play and, if not given the right amount of appropriate toys and good training, can be destructive.

1. What is the farthest range of a dog's hearing?

   A. 2.5 yards
   B. 25 yards
   C. 250 yards
   D. 2500 yards

2 The author included the last paragraph in order to

   A. review the kinds of dogs mentioned earlier.
   B. tell the reader what to do after getting a dog.
   C. give the reader a reason to study dogs further.
   D. persuade the reader to research kinds of dogs.

3. According to the passage, which kind of dog would be a good fit for a person with a lot of energy but not a lot of space?

   A. Miniature Poodle
   B. Jack Russell Terrier
   C. Rottweiler
   D. Boston Terrier

4. What would be the **best** way to tell whether a dog is sick or not?

   A. see if the dog's nose is hot and dry
   B. see if the dog shows a change in behavior
   C. see if the dog lies around the house all day
   D. see if the dog's nose is wet

5. You live in an apartment with two small children and an elderly grandparent. Describe the ideal qualities of a dog you would like to adopt.

from "THIS SIDE OF PARADISE"

by F. Scott Fitzgerald

CHAPTER 1: AMORY, SON OF BEATRICE

Amory Blaine inherited from his mother every trait, except the stray inexpressible few, that made him worth while. His father, an ineffectual, inarticulate man with a taste for Byron and a habit of drowsing over the *Encyclopedia Britannica*, grew wealthy at thirty through the death of two elder brothers, successful Chicago brokers, and in the first flush of feeling that the world was his, went to Bar Harbor and met Beatrice O'Hara. In consequence, Stephen Blaine handed down to posterity his height of just under six feet and his tendency to waver at crucial moments, these two abstractions appearing in his son Amory. For many years he hovered in the background of his family's life, an unassertive figure with a face half-obliterated by lifeless, silky hair, continually occupied in "taking care" of his wife, continually harassed by the idea that he didn't and couldn't understand her.

But Beatrice Blaine! There was a woman! Early pictures taken on her father's estate at Lake Geneva, Wisconsin, or in Rome at the Sacred Heart Convent—an educational extravagance that in her youth was only for the daughters of the exceptionally wealthy—showed the exquisite delicacy of her features, the consummate art and simplicity of her clothes. A brilliant education she had—her youth passed in renaissance glory, she was versed in the latest gossip of the Older Roman Families; known by name as a fabulously wealthy American girl to Cardinal Vitori and Queen Margherita and more subtle celebrities that one must have had some culture even to have heard of. She learned in England to prefer whiskey and soda to wine, and her small talk was broadened in two senses during a winter in Vienna. All in all Beatrice O'Hara absorbed the sort of education that will be quite impossible ever again; a tutelage measured by the number of things and people one could be contemptuous of and charming about; a culture rich in all arts and traditions, barren of all ideas, in the last of those days when the great gardener clipped the inferior roses to produce one perfect bud.

In her less important moments she returned to America, met Stephen Blaine and married him—this almost entirely because she was a little bit weary, a little bit sad. Her only child was carried through a tiresome season and brought into the world on a spring day in ninety-six.

When Amory was five he was already a delightful companion for her. He was an auburn-haired boy, with great, handsome eyes which he would grow up to in time, a facile imaginative mind and a taste for fancy dress. From his fourth to his tenth year he did the country with his mother in her father's private car, from Coronado, where his mother became so bored that she had a nervous breakdown in a fashionable hotel, down to Mexico City, where she took a mild, almost epidemic consumption. This trouble pleased her, and later she made use of it as an intrinsic part of her atmosphere—especially after several astounding bracers.

So, while more or less fortunate little rich boys were defying governesses on the beach at Newport, or being spanked or tutored or read to from "Do and Dare," or "Frank on the

Mississippi," Amory was biting acquiescent bell-boys in the Waldorf, outgrowing a natural repugnance to chamber music and symphonies, and deriving a highly specialized education from his mother.

"Amory."

"Yes, Beatrice." (Such a quaint name for his mother; she encouraged it.)

"Dear, don't *think* of getting out of bed yet. I've always suspected that early rising in early life makes one nervous. Clothilde is having your breakfast brought up."

"All right."

"I am feeling very old to-day, Amory," she would sigh, her face a rare cameo of pathos, her voice exquisitely modulated, her hands as facile as Bernhardt's. "My nerves are on edge—on edge. We must leave this terrifying place to-morrow and go searching for sunshine."

Amory's penetrating green eyes would look out through tangled hair at his mother. Even at this age he had no illusions about her.

"Amory."

"Oh, *yes*."

"I want you to take a red-hot bath as hot as you can bear it, and just relax your nerves. You can read in the tub if you wish."

She fed him sections of the "Fêtes Galantes" before he was ten; at eleven he could talk glibly, if rather reminiscently, of Brahms and Mozart and Beethoven. One afternoon, when left alone in the hotel at Hot Springs, he sampled his mother's apricot cordial, and as the taste pleased him, he became quite tipsy. This was fun for a while, but he essayed a cigarette in his exaltation, and succumbed to a vulgar, plebeian reaction. Though this incident horrified Beatrice, it also secretly amused her and became part of what in a later generation would have been termed her "line."

"This son of mine," he heard her tell a room full of awestruck, admiring women one day, "is entirely sophisticated and quite charming—but delicate—we're all delicate; *here*, you know." Her hand was radiantly outlined against her beautiful bosom; then sinking her voice to a whisper, she told them of the apricot cordial. They rejoiced, for she was a brave raconteuse, but many were the keys turned in sideboard locks that night against the possible defection of little Bobby or Barbara. . . .

These domestic pilgrimages were invariably in state; two maids, the private car, or Mr. Blaine when available, and very often a physician. When Amory had the whooping-cough four disgusted specialists glared at each other hunched around his bed; when he took scarlet fever the number of attendants, including physicians and nurses, totaled fourteen.

However, blood being thicker than broth, he was pulled through. . . .

Amory became thirteen, rather tall and slender, and more than ever on to his Celtic mother. He had tutored occasionally—the idea being that he was to "keep up," at each place "taking up the work where he left off," yet as no tutor ever found the place he left off, his mind was still in very good shape. What a few more years of this life would have made of him is problematical. However, four hours out from land, Italy bound, with Beatrice, his appendix burst, probably from too many meals in bed, and after a series of frantic telegrams to Europe and America, to the amazement of the passengers the great ship slowly wheeled around and returned to New York to deposit Amory at the pier. You will admit that if it was not life it was magnificent.

After the operation Beatrice had a nervous breakdown that bore a suspicious resemblance to delirium tremens, and Amory was left in Minneapolis, destined to spend the ensuing two years with his aunt and uncle. There the crude, vulgar air of Western civilization first catches him—in his underwear, so to speak.

* * * *

A KISS FOR AMORY

His lip curled when he read it.

> *"I am going to have a bobbing party,"* it said, *"on Thursday, December the seventeenth, at five o'clock, and I would like it very much if you could come.*
>
> *Yours truly,*
> *R.S.V.P.*
> *Myra St. Claire."*

He had been two months in Minneapolis, and his chief struggle had been the concealing from "the other guys at school" how particularly superior he felt himself to be, yet this conviction was built upon shifting sands. He had shown off one day in French class (he was in senior French class) to the utter confusion of Mr. Reardon, whose accent Amory damned contemptuously, and to the delight of the class. Mr. Reardon, who had spent several weeks in Paris ten years before, took his revenge on the verbs, whenever he had his book open. But another time Amory showed off in history class, with quite disastrous results, for the boys there were his own age, and they shrilled innuendoes at each other all the following week:

"Aw—I b'lieve, doncher know, the Umuricun revolution was *lawgely* an affair of the middul *clawses*," or "Washington came of very good blood—aw, quite good—I b'lieve."

Amory ingeniously tried to retrieve himself by blundering on purpose. Two years before he had commenced a history of the United States which, though it only got as far as the Colonial Wars, had been pronounced by his mother completely enchanting.

His chief disadvantage lay in athletics, but as soon as he discovered that it was the touchstone of power and popularity at school, he began to make furious, persistent efforts to excel in the winter sports, and with his ankles aching and bending in spite of his efforts, he skated valiantly around the Lorelie rink every afternoon, wondering how soon he would be able to carry a hockey-stick without getting it inexplicably tangled in his skates.

The invitation to Miss Myra St. Claire's bobbing party spent the morning in his coat pocket, where it had an intense physical affair with a dusty piece of peanut brittle. During the afternoon he brought it to light with a sigh, and after some consideration and a preliminary draft in the back of Collar and Daniel's "First-Year Latin," composed an answer:

Dear Miss St. Claire:

Your truly charming envitation for the evening of next Thursday evening was truly delightful to receive this morning. I will be charm and inchanted indeed to present my compliments on next Thursday evening.

Faithfully,
Amory Blaine.

* * * *

On Thursday, therefore, he walked pensively along the slippery, shovel-scraped sidewalks, and came in sight of Myra's house, on the half-hour after five, a lateness which he fancied his mother would have favored. He waited on the door-step with his eyes nonchalantly half-closed, and planned his entrance with precision. He would cross the floor, not too hastily, to Mrs. St. Claire, and say with exactly the correct modulation:

"My *dear* Mrs. St. Claire, I'm *frightfully* sorry to be late, but my maid"—he paused there and realized he would be quoting—"but my uncle and I had to see a fella—Yes, I've met your enchanting daughter at dancing-school."

Then he would shake hands, using that slight, half-foreign bow, with all the starchy little females, and nod to the fellas who would be standing 'round, paralyzed into rigid groups for mutual protection.

A butler (one of the three in Minneapolis) swung open the door. Amory stepped inside and divested himself of cap and coat. He was mildly surprised not to hear the shrill squawk of conversation from the next room, and he decided it must be quite formal. He approved of that—as he approved of the butler.

"Miss Myra," he said.

To his surprise the butler grinned horribly.

"Oh, yeah," he declared, "she's here." He was unaware that his failure to be cockney was ruining his standing. Amory considered him coldly.

"But," continued the butler, his voice rising unnecessarily, "she's the only one what *is* here. The party's gone."

Amory gasped in sudden horror.

"What?"

"She's been waitin' for Amory Blaine. That's you, ain't it? Her mother says that if you showed up by five-thirty you two was to go after 'em in the Packard."

Amory's despair was crystallized by the appearance of Myra herself, bundled to the ears in a polo coat, her face plainly sulky, her voice pleasant only with difficulty.

"Lo, Amory."

"Lo, Myra." He had described the state of his vitality.

"Well—you *got* here, *any*ways."

"Well—I'll tell you. I guess you don't know about the auto accident," he romanced.

Myra's eyes opened wide.

"Who was it to?"

"Well," he continued desperately, "uncle 'n aunt 'n I."

"Was any one *killed*?"

Amory paused and then nodded.

"Your uncle?"—alarm.

"Oh, no just a horse—a sorta gray horse."

At this point the Erse butler snickered.

"Probably killed the engine," he suggested. Amory would have put him on the rack without a scruple.

"We'll go now," said Myra coolly. "You see, Amory, the bobs were ordered for five and everybody was here, so we couldn't wait—"

"Well, I couldn't help it, could I?"

"So mama said for me to wait till ha'past five. We'll catch the bobs before it gets to the

Minnehaha Club, Amory."

Amory's shredded poise dropped from him. He pictured the happy party jingling along snowy streets, the appearance of the limousine, the horrible public descent of him and Myra before sixty reproachful eyes, his apology—a real one this time. He sighed aloud.

"What?" inquired Myra.

"Nothing. I was just yawning. Are we going to *surely* catch up with 'em before they get there?" He was encouraging a faint hope that they might slip into the Minnehaha Club and meet the others there, be found in blase seclusion before the fire and quite regain his lost attitude.

"Oh, sure Mike, we'll catch 'em all right—let's hurry."

He became conscious of his stomach. As they stepped into the machine he hurriedly slapped the paint of diplomacy over a rather box-like plan he had conceived. It was based upon some "trade-lasts" gleaned at dancing-school, to the effect that he was "awful good-looking and *English*, sort of."

"Myra," he said, lowering his voice and choosing his words carefully, "I beg a thousand pardons. Can you ever forgive me?" She regarded him gravely, his intent green eyes, his mouth, that to her thirteen-year-old, arrow-collar taste was the quintessence of romance.

Yes, Myra could forgive him very easily.

"Why—yes—sure."

He looked at her again, and then dropped his eyes. He had lashes.

"I'm awful," he said sadly. "I'm diff'runt. I don't know why I make faux pas. 'Cause I don't care, I s'pose." Then, recklessly: "I been smoking too much. I've got t'bacca heart."

Myra pictured an all-night tobacco debauch, with Amory pale and reeling from the effect of nicotined lungs. She gave a little gasp.

"Oh, *Amory*, don't smoke. You'll stunt your *growth*!"

"I don't care," he persisted gloomily. "I gotta. I got the habit. I've done a lot of things that if my fambly knew"—he hesitated, giving her imagination time to picture dark horrors—"I went to the burlesque show last week."

Myra was quite overcome. He turned the green eyes on her again. "You're the only girl in town I like much," he exclaimed in a rush of sentiment. "You're simpatico."

Myra was not sure that she was, but it sounded stylish though vaguely improper.

Thick dusk had descended outside, and as the limousine made a sudden turn she was jolted against him; their hands touched.

"You shouldn't smoke, Amory," she whispered. "Don't you know that?"

He shook his head.

"Nobody cares."

Myra hesitated.

"*I* care."

Something stirred within Amory.

"Oh, yes, you do! You got a crush on Froggy Parker. I guess everybody knows that."

"No, I haven't," very slowly.

A silence, while Amory thrilled. There was something fascinating about Myra, shut away here cosily from the dim, chill air. Myra, a little bundle of clothes, with strands of yellow hair curling out from under her skating cap.

"Because I've got a crush, too—" He paused, for he heard in the distance the sound of young laughter, and, peering through the frosted glass along the lamp-lit street, he made out the dark outline of the bobbing party. He must act quickly. He reached over with a violent, jerky effort, and clutched Myra's hand—her thumb, to be exact.

"Tell him to go to the Minnehaha straight," he whispered. "I wanta talk to you—I *got* to talk to you."

Myra made out the party ahead, had an instant vision of her mother, and then—alas for convention—glanced into the eyes beside. "Turn down this side street, Richard, and drive straight to the Minnehaha Club!" she cried through the speaking tube. Amory sank back against the cushions with a sigh of relief.

"I can kiss her," he thought. "I'll bet I can. I'll *bet* I can!"

Overhead the sky was half crystalline, half misty, and the night around was chill and vibrant with rich tension. From the Country Club steps the roads stretched away, dark creases on the white blanket; huge heaps of snow lining the sides like the tracks of giant moles. They lingered for a moment on the steps, and watched the white holiday moon.

"Pale moons like that one"—Amory made a vague gesture—"make people mysterieuse. You look like a young witch with her cap off and her hair sorta mussed"—her hands clutched at her hair—"Oh, leave it, it looks *good*."

They drifted up the stairs and Myra led the way into the little den of his dreams, where a cosy fire was burning before a big sink-down couch. A few years later this was to be a great stage for Amory, a cradle for many an emotional crisis. Now they talked for a moment about bobbing parties.

"There's always a bunch of shy fellas," he commented, "sitting at the tail of the bob, sorta lurkin' an' whisperin' an' pushin' each other off. Then there's always some crazy cross-eyed girl"—he gave a terrifying imitation—"she's always talkin' *hard*, sorta, to the chaper-on."

"You're such a funny boy," puzzled Myra.

"How d'y' mean?" Amory gave immediate attention, on his own ground at last.

"Oh—always talking about crazy things. Why don't you come ski-ing with Marylyn and I to-morrow?"

"I don't like girls in the daytime," he said shortly, and then, thinking this a bit abrupt, he added: "But I like you." He cleared his throat. "I like you first and second and third."

Myra's eyes became dreamy. What a story this would make to tell Marylyn! Here on the couch with this *wonderful*-looking boy—the little fire—the sense that they were alone in the great building—

Myra capitulated. The atmosphere was too appropriate.

"I like you the first twenty-five," she confessed, her voice trembling, "and Froggy Parker twenty-sixth."

Froggy had fallen twenty-five places in one hour. As yet he had not even noticed it.

But Amory, being on the spot, leaned over quickly and kissed Myra's cheek. He had never kissed a girl before, and he tasted his lips curiously, as if he had munched some new fruit.

Then their lips brushed like young wild flowers in the wind.

"We're awful," rejoiced Myra gently. She slipped her hand into his, her head drooped against his shoulder. Sudden revulsion seized Amory, disgust, loathing for the whole incident. He desired frantically to be away, never to see Myra again, never to kiss any one; he became conscious of his face and hers, of their clinging hands, and he wanted to creep out of his body and hide somewhere safe out of sight, up in the corner of his mind.

"Kiss me again." Her voice came out of a great void.

"I don't want to," he heard himself saying. There was another pause.

"I don't want to!" he repeated passionately.

Myra sprang up, her cheeks pink with bruised vanity, the great bow on the back of her head trembling sympathetically.

"I hate you!" she cried. "Don't you ever dare to speak to me again!"

"What?" stammered Amory.

"I'll tell mama you kissed me! I will too! I will too! I'll tell mama, and she won't let me play with you!"

Amory rose and stared at her helplessly, as though she were a new animal of whose presence on the earth he had not heretofore been aware.

The door opened suddenly, and Myra's mother appeared on the threshold, fumbling with her lorgnette.

"Well," she began, adjusting it benignantly, "the man at the desk told me you two children were up here—How do you do, Amory."

Amory watched Myra and waited for the crash—but none came. The pout faded, the high pink subsided, and Myra's voice was placid as a summer lake when she answered her mother.

"Oh, we started so late, mama, that I thought we might as well—"

He heard from below the shrieks of laughter, and smelled the vapid odor of hot chocolate and tea-cakes as he silently followed mother and daughter down-stairs. The sound of the graphophone mingled with the voices of many girls humming the air, and a faint glow was born and spread over him:

> *"Casey-Jones—mounted to the cab-un*
> *Casey-Jones—'th his orders in his hand.*
> *Casey-Jones—mounted to the cab-un*
> *Took his farewell journey to the prom-ised land."*

1. Why does Beatrice marry Stephen?

A. She is in love with him.
B. Her father likes Stephen.
C. She is feeling weary and sad.
D. He wants a home and a family.

2. How does Beatrice feel about Amory?

A. She is amused by him.
B. She is annoyed with him.
C. She is bored by him.
D. She is angry with him.

3. What causes Beatrice to leave Amory with his aunt and uncle?

A. She wants to spend more time with her husband.
B. She needs to care for her sick parents.
C. She has been offered a job outside the country.
D. She becomes too nervous to care for him.

4. What is the **major** conflict in the second part of this passage?

A. Amory disagrees with his mother's ideas about education.
B. Amory doesn't like living with his aunt and uncle.
C. Amory doesn't fit in with the other kids at school.
D. Amory misses spending time with his mother and father.

5. How does Amory try to become more popular?

A. He shows off in French class.
B. He decides to learn how to play a sport.
C. He shows them pictures from his travels.
D. He decides to throw a bobbing party.

6. Read the sentence below from the story.

Then he would shake hands, using that slight, half-foreign bow, with all the starchy little females, and nod to the fellas who would be standing 'round, paralyzed into rigid groups for <u>mutual</u> protection.

In the sentence, the word <u>mutual</u> probably means

A. weaker.
B. united.
C. physical.
D. surprising.

7. How do the other children in the story treat Amory?

A. They accept him.
B. They frighten him.
C. They tease him.
D. They ignore him.

8. Why does Amory show up late for Myra's party?

A. His uncle has to meet someone before taking him.
B. His aunt does not want him to go to the party.
C. His mother would have approved of being late.
D. He was stuck in a traffic jam outside of town.

9. Why does Amory pretend to admire Myra?

A. He does not want to see the other children.
B. He does not want her mother to be mad.
C. She is very hurt that he is late to her party.
D. She tells him that he likes her first.

10. Do you think you would have enjoyed growing up the way Amory did? Why or why not? Use details from the story to support your answer.

No, I would'nt really enjoy growing up the way Amory did because ~~he~~ his mother was to nervous to take care of Amory so he had to live with his aunt and uncle. In the story it seemed that nobody really cared about him which meant he had no support and had to live for himself. Since he made his own decisions he did'nt know what ~~is~~ was right or wrong so he began a habit of smoking which does'nt sound like a pleasant childhood and growing up.

11. Describe a time when you had to make a difficult adjustment. Compare your adjustment to Amory's. Use details from the story to support your answer.

I had to make an adjustment and live with lizards, cold water and hot weather in Pakistan for two-month's. My experience was really different to my regular lifestyle here. in Canada.,

Amory had to make his own ~~desicion~~ decisions and live with his aunt and uncle which seems different with living with his mother.

ROCK AND ROLL

By the early 1950s, jazz had lost some of its appeal to a mass audience. A new form of pop music, "rock and roll," evolved from an African American style known as "rhythm and blues." These were songs with strong beats and often risqué lyrics.

Though written by and for African Americans, rhythm and blues also appealed to white teenagers. Listening to it over radio stations geared toward African American listeners late at night became a secret pleasure. To make the new music more acceptable to a mainstream audience, white performers and arrangers began to "cover" rhythm-and-blues songs. The white singers performed them with the beat toned down and the lyrics cleaned up. A typical example is "Ain't That a Shame." It was a 1955 hit in a rock version by its black composer, Antoine "Fats" Domino. They became an even bigger hit as a ballad-like cover by a white performer, Pat Boone.

Shrewd record producers of the time realized that a magnetic white man who could sing with the energy of a African American man would have enormous appeal. Just such a figure appeared in the person of Elvis Presley. He had grown up poor in the south. Besides an emotional singing voice, Presley had sultry good looks. He also had a way of shaking his hips that struck adults as obscene but to teenagers it was natural to rock and roll. At first, Presley covered songs by black singers. One of his first big hits was "Hound Dog." It had been sung by blues artist "Big Mama" Thornton. Soon, however, Presley was singing original material, supplied by a new breed of rock-and-roll songwriters.

A few years after its debut, rock and roll was well on its way to becoming the American form of pop music, especially among the young. It spread quickly to Great Britain where the Beatles and the Rolling Stones started performing in the early 1960s.

1. In the third paragraph, the word <u>obscene</u> probably means

   A. indecent.
   B. distracting.
   C. confusing.
   D. distinguished.

2. Which **best** summarizes the passage?

   A. A new type of music called “rock and roll” was developed during the 1950s.
   B. “Rock and roll” is a type of music that includes strong beats and racy lyrics.
   C. In “rock and roll,” covering a song means recording a new version of the song.
   D. Elvis Presley’s first “rock and roll” hit was “Hound Dog” by “Big Mama” Thornton.

3. Using details from the passage, explain the origins of “rock and roll” music.

It was created by the africant americans to entertain. And it was called rytum and blues

Reproducing copyrighted material is against the law!

CHIEF JOSEPH

Chief Joseph had a claim to the Wallowa Valley in Oregon. It dated from the Stevens treaty in 1855. President Grant conceded it to him again in 1873. Two years later the concession was revoked. The Wallowa Valley was thrown into the public domain. Anyone could move in. All of Oregon west of the Snake River was opened up.

In 1877, it was determined to remove the Nez Perce from Oregon. They were to be sent to a reservation in Idaho. However, Chief White Bird sent word that he would not be removed. He and his people did not want to be put on a reservation. The Nez Perce decided to escape to Canada. The army tried to stop them. An unequal war began. It was between retreating bands of Nez Perce and companies of United States cavalry.

The American Indians crossed through Yellowstone Park. They crossed the Yellowstone River. They were closely followed by the army. In the battle that ensued near the mouth of Eagle Creek, six chiefs and 25 warriors were killed. Thirty-eight men were wounded. For the army, two officers and 21 men were killed. Four officers and 38 men were wounded. The whole camp of about 450 men, women, and children fell into Colonel Miles' hands. General Howard reached the battlefield just in time to be present at the surrender.

Chief Joseph conducted this retreat with very extraordinary skill. He beat Colonel Gibbon. Gibbon had 15 officers, 146 troopers, and 34 volunteers. He stampeded General Howard's horses and pack train. He fought Colonel Sturgis on the Yellowstone River and almost won. Chief Joseph came very close to making good his retreat to British America.

Of this campaign General Sherman has said the following:

> The [American] Indians throughout displayed a courage and skill that elicited universal praise. They abstained from scalping. They let captive women go free. They did not commit indiscriminate murder of peaceful families, which is usual. They fought with almost scientific skill, using advance and rear guards, skirmish lines, and field fortifications.

1. What caused the army go to war with the Nez Perce?

   A. The Nez Perce did not want to join the United States cavalry.
   B. The Nez Perce had broken the Stevens Treaty.
   C. The Nez Perce did not want to go to a reservation in Idaho.
   D. The Nez Perce had injured Colonel Gibbon.

2. Read the sentence below from the passage.

   Two years later the <u>concession</u> was revoked.

   In the sentence, the word <u>concession</u> probably means

   A. grant.
   B. land.
   C. reservation.
   D. president.

3. Which statement **best** describes Chief Joseph?

   A. He was a cruel man who wanted revenge on the army.
   B. He was curious as to why the Nez Perce had to leave Oregon.
   C. He was determined to get the Nez Perce people to safety.
   D. He was frightened by an attack of the American army.

4. Who had the **most** casualties in the battle at Eagle Creek? What was the likely result for the Nez Perce?

The American side had more casulties. This number was not anticipated since They had the upper hand in tools, money and men. This event was unlikely.

THE HOUSE WITH NOBODY IN IT

by Joyce Kilmer

Whenever I walk to Suffern along the Erie track
I go by a poor old farmhouse with its shingles broken and black.
I suppose I've passed it a hundred times, but I always stop for a minute
And look at the house, the tragic house, the house with nobody in it.

I never have seen a haunted house, but I hear there are such things;
That they hold the talk of spirits, their mirth and sorrowings.
I know this house isn't haunted, and I wish it were, I do;
For it wouldn't be so lonely if it had a ghost or two.

This house on the road to Suffern needs a dozen panes of glass,
And somebody ought to weed the walk and take a scythe to the grass.
It needs new paint and shingles, and the vines should be trimmed and tied;
But what it needs the most of all is some people living inside.

If I had a lot of money and all my debts were paid
I'd put a gang of men to work with brush and saw and spade.
I'd buy that place and fix it up the way it used to be
And I'd find some people who wanted a home and give it to them free.

Now, a new house standing empty, with staring window and door,
Looks idle, perhaps, and foolish, like a hat on its block in the store.
But there's nothing mournful about it; it cannot be sad and lone
For the lack of something within it that it has never known.

But a house that has done what a house should do, a house that has sheltered life,
That has put its loving wooden arms around a man and his wife,
A house that has echoed a baby's laugh and held up his stumbling feet,
Is the saddest sight, when it's left alone, that ever your eyes could meet.

So whenever I go to Suffern along the Erie track
I never go by the empty house without stopping and looking back,
Yet it hurts me to look at the crumbling roof and the shutters fallen apart,
For I can't help thinking the poor old house is a house with a broken heart.

1. What is the **major** conflict in the poem?

A. The speaker cannot seem to sell the old house to anyone.
B. The speaker is unable to fix up the house and give it away.
C. The speaker is haunted by the ghosts living in the old house.
D. The speaker feels bad that he has to leave his old home.

2. Read the lines below from the poem.

"But a house that has done what a house should do, a house that has sheltered life,/ That has put its loving wooden arms around a man and his wife,"

The sentence contains an example of which type of figurative language?

A. personification
B. hyperbole
C. metaphor
D. simile

3. What does the speaker believe is the purpose of a house?

A. to shelter life
B. to make families happy
C. to look nice
D. to give people a place to sleep

4. What does the speaker believe would make the house feel better?

A. a ghost haunting it
B. tearing it down
C. a parade going by
D. building a new house next door

5. Which word **best** describes the empty house in the poem?

A. bitter
B. lonely
C. anxious
D. gentle

6. How is an empty new house **different** from an empty old house?

A. An empty new house is a better place to raise children.
B. An empty new house feels good because it looks good.
C. An empty new house doesn't know that it is missing love.
D. An empty new house doesn't have all of its windows and doors.

LASER EYE SURGERY

Laser eye surgery is intended for people who want to minimize their dependency on glasses or contact lenses. Laser surgery can provide vision correction similar to what would be obtained with glasses or contact lenses.

The greatest interest has been in a procedure popularly known as LASIK. Advertising for this technique appears prominently on broadcast outlets. Fortunately, most surgeons and medical centers are doing a good job of educating the public about the risks and benefits of LASIK.

LASIK permanently changes the shape of the cornea. It is performed for varying degrees of nearsightedness, farsightedness, and astigmatism. A surgical knife is used to cut a flap in the cornea. A hinge is left at one end of the flap. The flap is then folded back to reveal the middle layer of the cornea. It is called the "stroma." Pulses from a computer-controlled excimer laser vaporize a portion of the stroma. The flap is then replaced. By removing this tissue, the shape of the central cornea is changed. The refractive error is reduced.

Doctors say that LASIK gives a rapid visual recovery, with minimal pain, and little or no post-operative discomfort. In fact, most people who undergo LASIK, like Beth Polazzo, can see well enough to drive immediately after surgery. They usually have excellent vision within a week.

"I had good vision immediately. This is the best I've seen since I was seven years old," reported Beth Polazzo.

The laser does its work on each eye in less than a minute. Patients are typically back to work or their normal activities within three days.

While most people are pleased with the results of their surgery, there are risks involved. Some suffer permanent loss of vision. Others have a reduction in the quality of vision. This may include the development of glare, halos, and starbursts. Some have difficulty with night driving. Others find reduced vision in dimly-lit conditions. These risks are doubled when both eyes are treated at the same time.

1. According to the passage, what is LASIK?

   A. a group of eye doctors
   B. a kind of contact lens
   C. a type of laser eye surgery
   D. a category of radio ad

2. Which of these is LASIK **most** likely to reduce?

   A. cataracts
   B. blindness
   C. nearsightedness
   D. ultraviolet rays

3. The author includes the information in the sixth paragraph in order to

   A. describe all the steps of the surgery.
   B. make the surgery sound uncomfortable.
   C. explain how surgeons educate people.
   D. identify the risks of the eye surgery.

4. The author's **main** purpose for writing the passage is to

   A. inform readers about a medical operation.
   B. convince readers to have laser eye surgery.
   C. warn readers about the dangers of eye surgery.
   D. entertain readers with a story about an eye doctor.

5. How would you **probably** advise a friend who is thinking of having laser surgery on both eyes at once? Identify and explain one piece of advice you would give to your friend.

EARTHQUAKES

Some people believe that, when the "Big One" hits, California will disappear. It will suddenly "break off" and "fall into the Pacific." Others believe that the earth will "open up" along the fault. It will "swallow" people, cars, and houses.

Such beliefs have no scientific basis whatsoever. Although ground slippage commonly takes place in a large earthquake, the earth will not open up. Nor will California fall into the sea. The San Andreas fault zone only extends a little more than nine miles (15 km) deep. That is only about a quarter of the thickness of the continental crust.

The San Andreas fault zone separates the Pacific and North American Plates. These plates are slowly grinding past each other in a roughly north-south direction. The Pacific Plate on the western side of the fault is moving horizontally in a northerly direction relative to the North American Plate on the eastern side of the fault.

Evidence of the sideways shift of these two land masses can be found all along the fault zone. It can be seen from the differences in topography and geologic structures. Sometimes it can even be seen in vegetation of the terrain from one side of the fault to the other.

Movement along the San Andreas fault zone can occur in sudden jolts. Or it can occur in a slow, steady motion called "creep." Fault segments that are actively creeping experience many small to moderate earthquakes that cause little or no damage.

These creeping segments are separated by segments of infrequent earthquake activity. These areas are stuck or locked in place within the fault zone. Locked segments of the fault store a tremendous amount of energy. Energy can build up for decades, or even centuries. Finally it is unleashed in massive earthquakes. For example, the Great San Francisco Earthquake was an 8.3-magnitude earthquake. In 1906, the earth ruptured along a previously locked segment of the San Andreas fault which measured slightly more than 267 miles (430 km) long.

1. What will **probably** happen when the "Big One" hits?

   A. California will break off and fall into the Pacific.
   B. A locked segment of earth will become unlocked.
   C. The earth will swallow people, cars, and houses.
   D. The earth will open up for miles along the fault.

2. The author included the information in the sixth paragraph in order to show readers that

   A. a large earthquake follows a period with no earthquakes.
   B. San Francisco was the site of a large earthquake in 1906.
   C. large earthquakes occur when too much energy builds up.
   D. pressure between plates can build for a very long time.

3. The purpose of listing several phrases in quotes in the first paragraph to

   A. show that they are important words.
   B. show that they are not scientific terms.
   C. tell the reader that those phrases are quotes.
   D. tell the reader to say those words out loud.

4. Describe what you might see on each side of the San Andreas Fault. Use details from the passage to support your answer.

Due to pushing of the plates toward each other, we are to most likely expiriance the view of a montain range. If you were to look at a map, you can see that they align with the rocky mountains as a boarder between plates. This is along the fault.

GEORGE WASHINGTON BUSH - Part I

George Washington Bush was born in the late 1700s. He was raised and educated by Quakers. An only child, he inherited enough from his parents to be financially independent. He served under Andrew Jackson at the Battle of New Orleans in 1815. Later he was among the first mountain men to trap in the Oregon Territory. Returning from the frontier in 1830, he married the daughter of a German Baptist minister. Over the next 11 years their farm north of Kansas City prospered.

In 1844, Michael Simmons, an Irish immigrant, asked Bush to help lead a group of 32 people to Oregon. Bush decided to serve not only as a guide but to become an emigrant himself. He gave up a comfortable home and life. He sold his farm and nearly all of his possessions. He readied his wife and five sons for the journey. He built a false floor into his wagon to hide more than $2,000 in silver coins. This hidden treasure allowed Bush to help others in the party who were not able to fully finance their journey.

On May 10, 1844, they began their journey west. Each day began at 4:00 a.m. The livestock were brought in from grazing, breakfast was eaten, camp struck, the teams hitched and the wagons were back on the trail before 6:00 a.m. At noon, they stopped for an hour or so to rest the stock, have dinner, and teach lessons to the children. Underway again by 1:00 p.m. they made camp before sundown. Each day they covered between 13 and 25 miles. Day after day, in the sun or rain, they choked on dust or pulled every step from boot-deep mud. They hauled themselves and all their belongings up and down steep ravines and they forded swollen streams.

By the time they reached Fort Bridger in the modern state of Wyoming, some of the group had run out of supplies and clothing. George Washington Bush bought flour, sugar and calico at wildly inflated prices. He did this so that all of the members of the group would be fed, clothed and supplied before they continued.

Thanks to the knowledge and experience of George Washington Bush, the wagon train arrived—after more than four months and 2,000 miles—in Oregon. At that time Oregon Territory was not yet part of the United States. U.S. settlers formed the Oregon Provisional Government. They passed their first code of laws in 1843.

All of the members of the Simmons-Bush party were welcomed to the new territory—all, that is, except George Washington Bush. Neither wealth nor friends could protect him from the provisional government's law prohibiting him from settling in Oregon. Bush was excluded for just one reason. It was the color of his skin. His father, Matthew Bush, was a black man.

Matthew Bush had been the lifelong servant of an English merchant named Stevenson. Stevenson settled in Philadelphia. He owned several ships there. Matthew Bush married an Irish maid of Stevenson's. Together they cared for Stevenson in his declining years. Since Stevenson had no children, he left a substantial fortune to Matthew Bush.

1. Why was George Washington Bush **probably** asked to lead a group to Oregon?

A. He had been a soldier.
B. He had been a mountain man.
C. He had a father who was black.
D. He was very wealthy.

2. Which sentence from the passage **best** supports the author's conclusion that Bush was a generous man?

A. He did this so that all of the members of the group were fed, clothed, and supplied before they continued.
B. Thanks to the knowledge and experience of George Washington Bush, the wagon train arrived...
C. He built a false floor into his wagon to hide more than $2,000 in silver coins.
D. An only child, he inherited enough from his parents to be financially independent.

3. In the sixth paragraph, the word <u>excluded</u> probably means

A. left out.
B. moved away.
C. protected from.
D. allowed in.

4. Do you think that the Oregon law was surprising for that time and place? Give one reason why you do or do not find the law surprising. Use details from the passage to support your answer.

In my opinion, this was not suprising. Since in the past people were racist, and black no, white of course, was the law. This is just a normal law for the time.

GEORGE WASHINGTON BUSH - Part II

The story of George Washington Bush might have ended when he tried to settle in Oregon but he was turned away. However, he had friends who exemplified the spirit of the West. The Simmons group was thankful for the gifts and assistance that George Washington Bush had given them during their western trek. The entire group agreed not to settle anywhere that Bush could not.

They spent their first winter on the northern bank of the Columbia River. They were about 20 miles east of present-day Portland. It was an area in which the British Hudson's Bay Company had previously prohibited American settlement. Oregon Territory laws were not enforced there. Dr. McLoughlin, the British agent at Fort Vancouver, was sympathetic to Bush's problem. He and his American Indian wife understood the ill effects of prejudice.

The small community supported itself by making and selling rough cedar shingles. They wanted to find a permanent location for a town. Bush accompanied Simmons to an area south of Puget Sound. He remembered the area from his trapping days. By October, 1845, the entire Simmons-Bush group had made a claim for lands just south of Olympia. The settlement became known as "Tumwater." Tumwater was the first permanent American settlement in what was to become the state of Washington. Its success encouraged others to follow.

Bush and Simmons built the area's first gristmill and sawmill. Bush helped to finance Simmons's logging company. Bush's compassion was substantial. He divided his crops with needy friends. He forged good relations with neighboring American Indians. Bush and his wife, Isabella, nursed American Indian people through epidemics of measles and smallpox.

In 1852 the grain supply was low on Puget Sound. Speculators tried to corner the entire wheat crop. They offered Bush a high price for his wheat. Bush told him that he would keep it "so my neighbors will have enough to live on and for seeding their fields in the spring. They have no money to pay your fancy prices. I don't intend to see them want for anything I can provide them." For the Bush family, the way was never too long or the night too stormy to come to the assistance of a neighbor.

An 1846 treaty moved the northern boundary of the Oregon Territory to the current northern boundary of the state of Washington. Again Bush's land claim was put into jeopardy. In 1853, Washington Territory was separated from Oregon. In 1854, a group of Bush's friends succeeded in passing a memorial through the Washington Territorial Legislature. It requested that the U.S. Congress grant the Bush family title to the land on which they had been living for nine years. In January 1855, Congress passed this special act, making it so.

George Washington Bush died in 1863 at the age of 84. He is the only veteran of the War of 1812 buried in Thurston County, Washington. Isabella died two years later. Their sons carried on their tradition of farming skills and public service. One, William Owen Bush, served twice in the Washington state legislature.

1. What caused the Simmons-Bush group to start its own settlement?

   A. The Oregon Territory had quickly become overcrowded.
   B. The settlers refused to live anywhere that Bush could not.
   C. The settlers wanted to live closer to the Puget Sound.
   D. The Oregon Territory had far too many laws to follow.

2. In the fourth paragraph, the word <u>epidemics</u> probably means

   A. outbreaks of illnesses.
   B. seasons of good weather.
   C. complex puzzles.
   D. long-fought battles.

3. The author's **main** purpose for writing the passage is to

   A. discuss the development of the Washington Territory.
   B. tell about the life of a great American pioneer.
   C. explain why people traveled to the West in the 1800s.
   D. describe how Bush had befriended the American Indians.

4. How did George Washington Bush help his friends and neighbors? Use details from the passage to support your answer.

5. How did his friends and neighbors help George Washington Bush? Use details from the passage to support your answer.

from "THE RED-HEADED LEAGUE"

by Arthur Conan Doyle

It was a quarter-past nine when I started from home and made my way across the Park, and so through Oxford Street to Baker Street. Two hansoms were standing at the door, and, as I entered the passage, I heard the sound of voices from above. On entering his room, I found Holmes in animated conversation with two men, one of whom I recognized as Peter Jones, the official police agent. The other was a long, thin, sad-faced man, with a very shiny hat and oppressively respectable frock coat.

"Ha! Our party is complete," said Holmes, buttoning up his pea-jacket, and taking his heavy hunting crop from the rack. "Watson, I think you know Mr. Jones, of Scotland Yard? Let me introduce you to Mr. Merryweather, who is to be our companion in to-night's adventure."

"We're hunting in couples again, doctor, you see," said Jones, in his consequential way. "Our friend here is a wonderful man for starting a chase. All he wants is an old dog to help him do the running down."

"I hope a wild goose may not prove to be the end of our chase," observed Mr. Merryweather gloomily.

"You may place considerable confidence in Mr. Holmes, sir," said the police agent loftily. "He has his own little methods, which are, if he won't mind my saying so, just a little too theoretical and fantastic, but he has the makings of a detective in him. It is not too much to say that once or twice, as in that business of the Sholto murder and the Agra treasure, he has been more nearly correct than the official force."

"Oh, if you say so, Mr. Jones, it is all right!" said the stranger, with deference. "Still, I confess that I miss my rubber. It is the first Saturday night for seven-and-twenty years that I have not had my rubber."

"I think you will find," said Sherlock Holmes, "that you will play for a higher stake to-night than you have ever done yet, and that the play will be more exciting. For you, Mr. Merryweather, the stake will be some 30,000 pounds; and for you, Jones, it will be the man upon whom you wish to lay your hands."

"John Clay, the murderer, thief, smasher, and forger. He's a young man, Mr. Merryweather, but he is at the head of his profession, and I would rather have my bracelets on him than on any criminal in London. He's a remarkable man, is young John Clay. His grandfather was a Royal Duke, and he himself has been to Eton and Oxford. His brain is as cunning as his fingers, and though we meet signs of him at every turn, we never know where to find the man himself. He'll crack a crib in Scotland one week, and be raising money to build an orphanage in Cornwall the next. I've been on his track for years, and have never set eyes on him yet."

"I hope that I may have the pleasure of introducing you to-night. I've had one or two little turns also with Mr. John Clay, and I agree with you that he is at the head of his profession. It is past ten, however, and quite time that we started. If you two will take the first hansom, Watson and I will follow in the second."

1. Read the sentence below from the passage.

   "I hope a wild goose may not prove to be the end of our chase..."

   The sentence is an example of which type of figurative language?

   A. onomatopoeia
   B. personification
   C. hyperbole
   D. metaphor

2. Why was John Clay difficult to catch?

   A. because he was hiding from Holmes
   B. because he was no longer involved in crime
   C. because he was fast and unpredictable
   D. because he was protected by Scotland Yard

3. In the fifth paragraph, the word <u>loftily</u> probably means

   A. highly
   B. overbearingly
   C. proudly
   D. remotely

4. Which sentence **best** summarizes the story?

   A. Four men discussed their plan to search for a criminal.
   B. Three men waited for a fourth man to arrive one night.
   C. Four men talked about what it takes to be a detective.
   D. Three men told a fourth man that he would be arrested.

5. What kind of a person was John Clay? Describe him using details from the story.

from "THE GARDENER' S SON"

Once upon a time in a certain country there lived a king whose palace was surrounded by a spacious garden. But, though the gardeners were many and the soil was good, this garden yielded neither flowers nor fruits, not even grass or shady trees.

The King was in despair about it, when a wise old man said to him: "Your gardeners do not understand their business. What can you expect of men whose fathers were cobblers and carpenters? How should they have learned to cultivate your garden?"

"You are quite right," cried the King.

"Therefore," continued the old man, "you should send for a gardener whose father and grandfather have been gardeners before him. Very soon your garden will be full of green grass and gay flowers, and you will enjoy its delicious fruit."

So the King sent messengers to every town, village, and hamlet in his dominions, to look for a gardener whose forefathers had also been gardeners. After 40 days one was found.

"Come with us and be gardener to the King," they said to him.

"How can I go to the King," said the gardener, "a poor wretch like me?"

"That is of no consequence," they answered. "Here are new clothes for you and your family."

"But I owe money to several people."

"We will pay your debts," they said.

So the gardener allowed himself to be persuaded, and went away with the messengers, taking his wife and his son with him. The King, delighted to have found a real gardener, entrusted him with the care of his garden. The man found no difficulty in making the royal garden produce flowers and fruit. At the end of a year the park was not like the same place. The King showered gifts upon his new servant.

The gardener, as you have heard already, had a son, who was a very handsome young man, with most agreeable manners. Every day he carried the best fruit of the garden to the King, and all the prettiest flowers to his daughter. Now this princess was wonderfully pretty and was just sixteen years old. The King was beginning to think it was time that she should be married.

"My dear child," said he, "you are of an age to take a husband, therefore I am thinking of marrying you to the son of my prime minister."

"Father," replied the Princess, "I will never marry the son of the minister."

"Why not?" asked the King.

"Because I love the gardener's son," answered the Princess.

On hearing this the King was at first very angry. Then he wept and sighed, and declared that such a husband was not worthy of his daughter. But the young Princess was not to be turned from her resolution to marry the gardener's son.

Then the King consulted his ministers. "This is what you must do," they said. "To get rid of the gardener you must send both suitors to a very distant country, and the one who returns first shall marry your daughter."

The King followed this advice. The minister's son was presented with a splendid horse and a purse full of gold pieces, while the gardener's son had only an old lame horse and a purse full of copper money, and everyone thought he would never come back from his journey.

The day before they started the Princess met her lover and said to him: "Be brave, and remember always that I love you. Take this purse full of jewels and make the best use you can of them for love of me, and come back quickly and demand my hand."

1. What is the **main** idea of the story?

   A. Flowers, trees, and even grass refused to grow in the King's palace garden.
   B. The King's assistants decided to find a gardener whose forefathers had been gardeners.
   C. The Princess falls in love with the gardener's son but the King wants to keep them from marrying.
   D. The King holds a contest to see which young man could ride to a distant land and return safely.

2. What is the **major** conflict in this story?

   A. The king's garden will not grow any fruit, flowers, or grass.
   B. The king does not want his daughter to marry the gardener's son.
   C. The gardener's son has nothing to give to the king's daughter.
   D. The gardener thinks that he is too poor to work for the king.

3. What will **probably** happen next in the story?

A. The Princess will marry the minister's son.
B. The gardener's son will stay in the distant land.
C. The King will decide to cancel the contest.
D. The gardener's son will win the contest.

4. Read the sentence below from the story

So the King sent messengers to every town, village, and hamlet in his <u>dominions</u>, to look for a gardener whose forefathers had also been gardeners.

In the sentence, the word <u>dominions</u> probably means

A. helpers.
B. castle.
C. powers.
D. kingdom.

5. Do you think that the princess's gift will be enough for the gardener's son to succeed? Explain why you think so, using details from the story.

from "ADVENTURE OF THE BLACK FISHERMAN"

by Washington Irving

When he woke all was quiet. The night was dark and moonless. From the state of the tide Sam concluded it was near midnight. He was on the point of making loose his skiff to return homeward when he saw a light gleaming along the water from a distance, which seemed rapidly approaching. As it drew near he perceived it came from a lantern in the bow of a boat gliding along under shadow of the land. It pulled up in a small cove close to where he was.

A man jumped on shore, and searching about with the lantern, exclaimed, "This is the place—here's the iron ring." The boat was then made fast, and the man, returning on board, assisted his comrades in conveying something heavy on shore. As the light gleamed among them, Sam saw that they were five stout, desperate-looking fellows, in red woolen caps, with a leader in a three-cornered hat. Some of them were armed with dirks, or long knives, and pistols. They talked low to one another, and occasionally in some outlandish tongue which he could not understand.

On landing they made their way among the bushes, taking turns to relieve each other in lugging their burden up the rocky bank. Sam's curiosity was now fully aroused, so leaving his skiff he clambered silently up a ridge that overlooked their path. They had stopped to rest for a moment, and the leader was looking about among the bushes with his lantern.

"Have you brought the spades?" said one.

"They are here," replied another, who had them on his shoulder.

"We must dig deep, where there will be no risk of discovery," said a third.

A cold chill ran through Sam's veins. He fancied he saw before him a gang of murderers, about to bury their victim. His knees smote together. In his agitation he shook the branch of a tree with which he was supporting himself as he looked over the edge of the cliff.

"What's that?" cried one of the gang. "Some one stirs among the bushes!"

The lantern was held up in the direction of the noise. One of the red-caps cocked a pistol, and pointed it toward the very place where Sam was standing. He stood motionless, breathless, expecting the next moment to be his last. Fortunately his dingy complexion was in his favor, and made no glare among the leaves.

" 'Tis no one," said the man with the lantern. "What a plague! You would not fire off your pistol and alarm the country!"

The pistol was uncocked, the burden was resumed, and the party slowly toiled along the bank. Sam watched them as they went, the light sending back fitful gleams through the dripping bushes, and it was not till they were fairly out of sight that he ventured to draw breath freely. He now thought of getting back to his boat, and making his escape out of the reach of such dangerous neighbors; but curiosity was all-powerful. He hesitated, and lingered, and listened. By and by he heard the strokes of spades. "They are digging the grave!" said he to himself, and the cold sweat started upon his forehead. Every stroke of a spade, as it sounded through the silent groves, went to his heart. It was evident there was as little noise made as possible; everything had an air of terrible mystery and secrecy. Sam had a great relish for the horrible; a tale of murder was a treat for him, and he was a constant attendant at executions. He could not resist an impulse, in spite of every danger, to steal nearer to the scene of mystery, and overlook the midnight fellows at their work. He crawled along cautiously, therefore, inch by inch, stepping with the utmost care among the dry leaves, lest their rustling should betray him. He came at length to where a steep rock intervened between him and the gang, for he saw the light of their lantern shining up against the branches of the trees on the other side. Sam slowly and silently clambered up the surface of the rock, and raising his head above its naked edge, beheld the villains immediately below him, and so near that though he dreaded discovery he dared not withdraw lest the least movement should be heard. In this way he remained, with his round black face peering above the edge of the rock, like the sun just emerging above the edge of the horizon, or the round-cheeked moon on the dial of a clock.

The red-caps had nearly finished their work, the grave was filled up, and they were carefully replacing the turf. This done they scattered dry leaves over the place. "And now," said the leader, "I defy the devil himself to find it out."

"The murderers!" exclaimed Sam involuntarily.

The whole gang started, and looking up beheld the round black head of Sam just above them, his white eyes strained half out of their orbits, his white teeth chattering, and his whole visage shining with cold perspiration.

"We're discovered!" cried one.

"Down with him!" cried another.

Sam heard the cocking of a pistol, but did not pause for the report. He scrambled over rock and stone, through brush and brier, rolled down banks like a hedgehog, scrambled up others like a catamount. In every direction he heard some one or other of the gang hemming him in. At length he reached the rocky ridge along the river; one of the red-caps was hard behind him. A steep rock like a wall rose directly in his way; it seemed to cut off all retreat, when fortunately he espied the strong, cord-like branch of a grapevine reaching half way down it. He sprang at it with the force of a desperate man, seized it with both hands, and, being young and agile, succeeded in swinging himself to the summit of the cliff. Here he stood in full relief against the sky, when the red-cap cocked his pistol and fired. The ball whistled by Sam's head. With the lucky thought of a man in an emergency, he uttered a yell, fell to the ground, and detached at the same time a fragment of the rock, which tumbled with a loud splash into the river.

"I've done his business," said the red-cap to one or two of his comrades as they arrived panting. "He'll tell no tales, except to the fishes in the river."

1. In the first paragraph, the word <u>perceived</u> probably means

   A. feared.
   B. guessed.
   C. wondered.
   D. noticed.

2. Which statement **best** describes Sam?

   A. He is a scholar.
   B. He is annoying.
   C. He is curious.
   D. He is a criminal.

3. What causes Sam to think that the men in the woods are murderers?

   A. They are burying a large trunk in the ground.
   B. They are carrying pistols with them.
   C. They are talking about the person that they killed.
   D. They are criminals that Sam knows.

4. Why did the red-cap think that Sam would tell tales only "to the fishes"? Use details from the story to support your answer.

WHY THE OPOSSUM' S TAIL IS BARE - Part I

A Cherokee Story

It must be remembered that the animals that appear in American Indian myths and legends are not the same as those that exist now. When the world began, animals were much bigger, stronger and cleverer than their present counterparts. Because of man's cruelty and aggression, these left the earth and took the rainbow path to Galunlati, the Sky Land, where they still remain. The animals that came after them are those we know today. They are but poor, weak imitations of those first creatures.

In the beginning, before this happened, all living things—men, animals, plants and trees—spoke the same language and behaved in much the same way. Animals, like people, were organized into tribes. They had chiefs, lived in houses, held councils and ceremonies.

Many animals had characteristics that we would not recognize today. The rabbit, for example, was fierce, bold and cunning, and a great mischief-maker. It was through Rabbit's tricks that the deer lost his sharp wolf-like teeth, the buzzard his handsome topknot of feathers, and the opossum his long, bushy tail.

Opossum was very proud of his tail which, in those days, was covered with thick black fur. He spent long hours cleaning and brushing it and composing songs about its beauty and vigor. Sometimes, when he walked through the village, he carried his tail erect, like a banner rippling in the breeze. At other times, he swept it low behind him, like a train. It was useful as well as beautiful, for when Opossum lay down to sleep, he tucked it under him to make a soft bed, and in cold weather he folded it over his body to keep himself warm.

Rabbit was very jealous of Opossum's tail. He, too, had once had a long bushy tail. During the course of a fight with Bear, he had lost most of it. Now he had only a short fluffy tuft. The sight of Opossum strutting before the other animals and swirling his tail ostentatiously, filled Rabbit with rage. He made up his mind to play a trick on him at the first opportunity.

At this time, when the animals still lived harmoniously together, each had his appointed station and duty. Thus, Frog was leader in the council and Rabbit, because of his speed, was employed to carry messages and announcements to the others.

1. The first paragraph is **mainly** about

A. how animals are weaker today than they were in the past.
B. how animals are smarter today than they were in the past.
C. why some animals have taken the rainbow path to Galunlati.
D. why some human beings have treated animals heartlessly.

2. Read the sentence below from the story.

Sometimes, when he walked through the village, he carried his tail erect, like a banner rippling in the breeze.

The sentence contains an example of which type of figurative language?

A. metaphor
B. simile
C. onomatopoeia
D. hyperbole

3. The animals of the past went to the Sky Land because

A. they had lost all of their brilliant traits.
B. humans chased them into the sky.
C. they had been punished for being vain.
D. humans had been violent toward them.

4. In the sixth paragraph, the word <u>harmoniously</u> probably means

   A. charmingly.
   B. quickly.
   C. peacefully.
   D. indifferently.

5. How did Rabbit lose **most** of his tail?

   A. as a messenger for Frog
   B. when he lost his teeth
   C. when Frog took it away
   D. in a conflict with Bear

6. Which word **best** describes how Rabbit felt about Opossum's tail?

   A. appreciative
   B. concerned
   C. resentful
   D. excited

7. What made Rabbit so mad at Opossum? Use details from the story to support your answer.

The reason is Jealosly.
Rabbit was Jealous that Mr. opossum had a useful, Attractive tail and he didn't. In this story it seem to be as if the opossum were to be flexing it's tail to the others in the animal kingdom. This made the Rabbit jealous, since, previously he lost his to bear.
The future parts of the story will most liklay be the opossum lost his tail and the Rabbit lost his life.

WHY THE OPOSSUM' S TAIL IS BARE - Part II

A Cherokee Story

As was their custom from time to time, the animals decided to hold a great council to discuss important matters. Rabbit, as usual, was given the task of arranging the gathering and delivering the invitations. Councils were also occasions for feasting and dancing. Rabbit saw a way of bringing about Opossum's downfall.

When Rabbit arrived with the news of the meeting, Opossum was sitting by the door of his lodge engaged in his favorite occupation—grooming his tail.

"I come to call you to the great council tomorrow, brother Opossum," said Rabbit. "Will you attend and join in the dance?"

"Only if I am given a special seat," replied the conceited Opossum, carefully smoothing some untidy hairs at the tip of his tail. "After all," he went on, grinning maliciously at Rabbit, "I have such a beautiful long tail that I ought to sit where everyone can see and admire it."

Bold word

Rabbit was almost beside himself with fury, but he pretended not to notice the jibe. He said, "But, of course, brother Opossum! I will personally see to it that you have the best seat in the council lodge. I will also send someone to dress your tail especially for the dance."

Opossum was delighted by this suggestion. Rabbit left him singing the praises of his tail even more loudly than usual. Next, Rabbit called on the cricket, whom American Indians call "the barber," because of his fame as an expert hair-cutter. Cricket listened with growing amazement as Rabbit recounted his conversation with Opossum. Like all the other animals, he found Opossum's vanity and arrogance very tiresome.

He began to protest. Rabbit held up a paw and said, "Wait a moment. I have a plan and I need your help. Listen . . . " and he dropped his voice as he told Cricket what he wanted him to do.

Early the next morning Cricket presented himself at Opossum's door. He said that he had been sent by Rabbit to prepare the famous tail for the council that evening. Opossum made himself comfortable on the floor and stretched out his tail. Cricket began to comb it gently.

"I will wrap this red cord round your tail as I comb it," he explained, "so that it will remain smooth and neat for the dance tonight."

Opossum found Cricket's ministrations so soothing that he fell asleep. He awakened just as Cricket was tying the final knot in the red cord that now completely swathed his tail.

“I will keep it bound up until the very last moment,” thought Opossum gleefully. “How envious the others will be when I finally reveal it in all its beauty!”

That evening, his tail still tightly wrapped in the red cord, Opossum marched into the council lodge. He was led to his special seat by a strangely obsequious Rabbit.

Soon it was time for the dancing to take place. The drums and rattles began to sound.

Opossum stood up and loosened the cord from his tail. He stepped proudly into the center of the dance floor. He began to sing.

“Look at my beautiful tail!” he sang as he circled the floor. “See how it sweeps the ground!”

There was a great shout from the audience and some of the animals began to applaud.

“How they admire me!” thought Opossum and he continued dancing and singing loudly. “See how my tail gleams in the firelight!”

Again everyone shouted and cheered. Opossum began to have just the merest suspicion that all was not quite as it should be. Was there possibly a hint of mockery in their voices? He dismissed such an absurd idea and continued dancing.

“My tail is stronger than the eagle’s, more lustrous than the raven’s!”

At this the animals shrieked so loudly that Opossum stopped in his tracks and looked at them. To his astonishment and chagrin they were all convulsed with laughter, some leaning weakly on their neighbor’s shoulders, others rolling on the ground in their mirth. Several were pointing at his tail.

Bewildered, Opossum looked down and saw to his horror that his tail, his beautiful, thick, glossy tail, was now black and scaly like that of a lizard. Nothing remained of its former glory. While pretending to comb it, the wily Cricket had snipped off every single hair.

Opossum was so overcome with shame and confusion that he could not utter a sound. Instead he rolled over helplessly on his back, grimacing with embarrassment, just as opossums still do today, when taken by surprise.

1. Read the sentence below from the story.

How <u>envious</u> the others will be when I finally reveal it in all its beauty!

In the sentence, the word <u>envious</u> probably means

A. joyful.
B. jealous.
C. entertaining.
D. modest.

2. How does Cricket feel about Opossum's tale?

A. He is appreciative of the care Opossum puts into his tail.
B. He doesn't think that Opossum's tail is long enough.
C. He doesn't think that Opossum's tail is very beautiful.
D. He is annoyed by all the attention Opossum pays to his tail.

3. How does Opossum act when Cricket offers to dress his tail?

A. cautious
B. irritated
C. delighted
D. indifferent

4. According to the passage, why do opossums play dead when attacked?

They play dead, in real life so that they don't get killed, or those left alone, According to the passage, the reason is to hide all that shame they kept their whole lives and not play dead so it wouldn't feel bad because they pretend dead. dead thing, don't feel any thing

"MENDING WALL"

by Robert Frost

When Robert Frost's father died in 1885, Robert was 11 years old. The family left California. They settled in Massachusetts. Frost attended Lawrence High School. He then entered Dartmouth College. He remained there less than one semester. Returning to Massachusetts, he taught school. He also worked in a mill and as a newspaper reporter.

From 1897 to 1899, Frost attended Harvard College as a special student. He left without a degree. Over the next 10 years he wrote (but rarely published) poems and operated a farm in Derry, New Hampshire. Frost supplemented his income by teaching at Pinkerton Academy.

Something there is that doesn't love a wall,
That sends the frozen-ground-swell under it
And spills the upper boulder in the sun,
And make gaps even two can pass abreast.
The work of hunters is another thing:
I have come after them and made repair
Where they have left not one stone on a stone,
But they would have the rabbit out of hiding,
To please the yelping dogs. The gaps I mean,
No one has seen them made or heard them made,
But at spring mending-time we find them there,
I let my neighbor know beyond the hill;
And on a day we meet to walk the line
And set the wall between us once again.
We keep the wall between us as we go.
To each the boulders that have fallen to each.
And some are loaves and some so nearly balls
We have to use a spell to make them balance:
"Stay where you are until our backs are turned!"
We wear our fingers rough with handling them.
Oh, just another kind of outdoor game,
One on a side. It comes to little more:
There where it is we do not need the wall:
He is all pine and I am apple orchard.
My apple trees will never get across
And eat the cones under his pines, I tell him.
He only says, "Good fences make good neighbors."
Spring is the mischief in me, and I wonder
If I could put a notion in his head:
"Why do they make good neighbors? Isn't it
Where there are cows? But here there are no cows.
Before I built a wall I'd ask to know

What I was walling in or walling out,
And to whom I was like to give offense.
Something there is that doesn't love a wall,
That wants it down." I could say "Elves" to him,
But it's not elves exactly, and I'd rather
He said it for himself. I see him there,
Bringing a stone grasped firmly by the top
In each hand, like an old-stone savage armed.
He moves in darkness as it seems to me,
Not of woods only and the shade of trees.
He will not go behind his father's saying,
And he likes having thought of it so well
He says again, "Good fences make good neighbors."

1. Read the lines below from the poem.

   Oh, just another kind of outdoor game / One on a side

   These lines contain an example of which type of figurative language?

   A. simile
   B. metaphor
   C. alliteration
   D. consonance

2. During which time of year do the speaker and his neighbor repair the wall?

   A. fall
   B. winter
   C. spring
   D. summer

3. What did the speaker and his neighbor do together?

   A. repair the wall
   B. cut down trees
   C. collect apples
   D. sit in the shade

4. After reading this poem, do you think that "good fences make good neighbors"? Explain why or why not.

HOW DO THEY DO IT?

A popular weight-loss myth is that everyone who loses weight eventually gains it back, says Rena Wing, Ph.D. She is a professor of psychiatry at Brown Medical School in Providence, Rhode Island. Wing, the co-developer of a research study known as the National Weight Control Registry, has worked to deflate this myth.

Tucked away in the registry's database is information about the weight-control behaviors of more than 3,000 American adults who have lost an average of 60 pounds and have kept it off for an average of six years.

How do they do it?

"These successful losers report four common behaviors," says Wing. "They eat a lowfat, high-carbohydrate diet. They monitor themselves by weighing in frequently. They are very physically active. They eat breakfast. Eating breakfast every day is contrary to the typical pattern for the average overweight person who is trying to diet."

"They get up in the morning and say 'I'm going to start my diet today.' They eat little or no breakfast and a light lunch. Then they get hungry and consume most of their calories late in the day. Successful weight losers have managed to change this pattern."

Six years after their weight loss, most of the registry's successful losers still report eating a low-calorie, lowfat diet, with about 24 percent of calories from fat. (The Dietary Guidelines for Americans recommend no more than 30 percent of daily calories from fat.) They also exercise for about an hour or more a day, expending about 2,800 calories per week on a variety of activities. "This is equivalent to walking 28 miles a week, or four miles a day," says Wing.

Wing also reports that more than 70 percent of the registry's weight losers became overweight before the age of 18.

Although Barbara Croft of Columbus, Ohio, was not an overweight child, she gained weight once she left home and started cooking for herself. Replacing the plain and simple meals she had as a child with pizza, sodas, and meat and vegetables laden with sauces, the five-foot-five-inch Croft worked her way up to 350 pounds.

"I always ate from all the food groups—I just ate huge portions and I ate in between meals," says Croft.

When she was diagnosed with Type 2 diabetes in February 1999, Croft got scared. "I worried about the health consequences—about going blind. I already have a little numbness in my feet."

Croft went on a diet and lost 200 pounds in 19 months. She has kept it off for a year and a half. “This is the third time I’ve lost over 100 pounds,” says the 52-year-old, 150-pound Croft, “but this is the longest I’ve been able to keep the weight off.”

In her two previous weight losses, Croft ate nutritious meals, but didn’t exercise. This time, she started walking for exercise, but could only walk about a block at first.

“My husband went with me because he was afraid I wouldn’t make it,” she says. Now, Croft walks on a treadmill for 50 minutes a day—25 minutes each morning and night.

She still eats balanced meals, but restricts her portions. And she always eats breakfast.

“I have Egg Beaters, two pieces of low-calorie bread, fruit, decaf coffee, and eight ounces of water.” Croft dines out almost every night, typically eating half her dinner of grilled chicken or salmon and a vegetable or salad. She sends the other half back, so she isn’t tempted to overeat.

“Losing the weight was easy—maintaining it is much harder,” says Croft.

Croft had tried commercial weight-loss programs in the past, but this last time she did it on her own. “You have to find out what works for you,” she says. “If I eat butter or cheese, that seems to do me in. Beef is also a problem.”

Croft’s diabetes is under control now without medication. And she says that her knees don’t hurt anymore. She can buy clothes in a regular store. Barbara Croft has started traveling again now that she can fit into an airplane seat.

1. This passage is **mainly** about

A. why eating breakfast is so important.
B. how dieters have kept the weight off.
C. how Barbara Croft finally lost weight.
D. the different diets used to lose weight.

2. What caused Barbara Croft to decide to lose weight again in 1999?

A. She was unable to walk very far.
B. She started to lose her sight.
C. She developed Type 2 diabetes.
D. She heard about Rena Wing's diet.

3. In the sixth paragraph, the word expending probably means

A. buying.
B. eating.
C. using.
D. lifting.

4. According to Rena Wing, what is the biggest mistake **most** dieters make?

A. eating high-fat foods
B. skipping exercise
C. eating too much at meals
D. skipping breakfast

5. How have Barbara Croft's diet plans changed over her three attempts? Does her latest diet seem successful?

ACTION PLANS KEEP ASTHMA IN CHECK

During the mid-1980s, Sandra Fusco-Walker's life was filled with sleepless nights. There were ruined vacations. She made lots of emergency room visits. Her children frequently missed activities. Her three children were all under the age of six at the time. Two of them had asthma.

"I was always worried about when the next bad thing would happen," says the Kinnelon, New Jersey resident. "But that was before we had a plan."

The "plan" was an asthma action plan. It guided her on how to track her children's symptoms, monitor their breathing, and give them medication.

"A plan tells you what to do and when," she says. "Without an action plan, asthma is out of control. That's when the disease wreaks havoc on your life."

Asthma causes the airways to be inflamed or swollen. When people with asthma react to various triggers, such as dust, pollen or smoke, their airways become narrow, which causes labored breathing, wheezing, chest tightness, or coughing. About 15 million people in the United States have asthma. Almost 5 million are children. Every year, asthma causes roughly 2 million emergency room visits, nearly 500,000 hospitalizations, and 4,500 deaths.

Fusco-Walker says she learned to control asthma after she followed her doctor's advice. She called a nonprofit organization called Allergy & Asthma Network Mothers of Asthmatics (AANMA). The woman who answered the phone was Nancy Sander. She had founded the organization in 1985 after facing challenges in dealing with her own daughter's asthma. Fusco-Walker says, "Nancy assured me that I wasn't going crazy."

With support and advice from AANMA, Fusco-Walker learned to look for patterns in her children's illness. For example, her kids got sick every time they visited her mother. Her mother smoked. Her oldest daughter had an asthma attack when she visited their horse barn. Fusco-Walker also learned to spot early warning signs of trouble.

"I noticed that one of my daughters rubbed her nose when breathing became difficult," she says. "If I saw her rubbing her nose, I knew to get the peak flow meter." A peak flow meter is a small tool that measures how fast air moves out of the airways. Fusco-Walker attributes the regular use of a peak flow meter to the success of her asthma action plan.

By the time Fusco-Walker's youngest child was diagnosed with asthma at the age of five, her family had a much better understanding of the disease. Shannon, who is now 16, Jared, 19, and Morgan, 21, grew up learning how to use their asthma medicine.

"They know when to use their inhalers, they know when they need refills, and they know when they need to take medication before doing an activity," she says. They also grew up participating in just about any activity they wanted to, including football, swimming, soccer, and snowboarding.

Experts say that most people with asthma can live normal, active lives. If you have asthma, you should avoid the triggers that make your asthma worse. You must keep track of your symptoms. You need to stick to an effective treatment regimen.

Many people with asthma need short-term medicine when they experience symptoms. They also need long-term daily medicine that reduces inflammation in the airways and helps prevent asthma attacks.

1. What **probably** the reason that Sandra Fusco-Walker created an asthma action plan?

   A. She was worried all the time.
   B. Her kids asked her to create one.
   C. She first learned about asthma.
   D. Her kids rubbed their noses.

2. The author's **main** purpose for writing the passage is to

   A. encourage readers to support asthma research.
   B. explain to readers what an asthma attack is like.
   C. describe how asthma affects children's lives.
   D. show how having a plan helps asthma patients.

3. The author included the quotation in the sixth paragraph in order to

   A. introduce AANMA founder Nancy Sander.
   B. show that Fusco-Walker had been upset.
   C. explain the mission of the AANMA.
   D. clarify that the chat took place in 1985.

4. How does asthma affect a person?

A

(A.) Asthma causes a person's airways to become inflamed.
~~B. Asthma reduces the speed at which a person's heart beats.~~
~~C. Asthma causes a person to feel sick to the stomach.~~
~~D. Asthma builds up fluids around a person's inner ear.~~

5. In the eighth paragraph, the word <u>attributes</u> probably means

(A.) blames.
B. records.
C. credits.
D. teaches.

6. How will Sandra Fusco-Walker **probably** feel the next time someone she loves has an asthma attack?

A. surprised
B. alarmed
(C.) prepared
D. nervous

7. Think about the plan that Sandra Fusco-Walker created for her children. Using details from the passage, describe an action plan for asthma.

If you are someone with asthma an action plan is a cheat code that helps, if you were to follow the plan. Almost a third of planet earth is affected By this sympton.

An action plan is a couple of Things/actions you do when asthma Kick in, using this you'll know the right time.

DESERT BIGHORN SHEEP

Bighorn are true sheep. They are distantly related to domestic sheep. The name "desert bighorn sheep" applies to those bighorn inhabiting hot and dry desert mountain ranges. These are ranges with sparse vegetation and water. Biologists recognize four races of desert bighorn. One race inhabits the Sonoran desert wilderness of the Cabeza Prieta in Arizona.

The desert bighorn has become well-adapted to living in the desert heat and cold. Unlike most mammals, their body temperature can safely fluctuate several degrees. During the heat of the day, bighorn often rest in the shade of trees and caves.

Cabeza Prieta's bighorn are typically found in small, scattered bands. They have adapted to a desert mountain environment. Bighorn feed on a wide variety of leaves, twigs, flowers, grasses, and cacti. They can live with little or no permanent water. Some of the bighorn may go for weeks or months without visiting one of the refuge's water developments. They sustain their body moisture from food and from rain water collected in temporary rock pools. They may have the ability to lose up to 30 percent of their body weight and still survive. After drinking water, they quickly recover from their dehydrated condition.

Wildlife ecologists are just beginning to study the importance of this adaptive strategy. It has allowed these small bands to survive in areas too dry for many of their predators.

Desert bighorn are stocky, heavy-bodied sheep. They are similar in size to mule deer. Weights of mature rams range from 125 to 200 pounds. Ewes are somewhat smaller. Due to their unique padded hooves, bighorn are able to climb the steep, rocky terrain of the desert mountains with speed and agility.

Bighorn rely on their keen eyesight to detect potential predators. Predators include mountain lions, coyotes, and bobcats. The bighorn use their climbing ability to escape.

Both sexes develop horns soon after birth. Horn growth continues throughout life. Older rams have impressive sets of curling horns. They measure over three feet long. They have more than one foot of circumference at the base.

Cabeza's bighorn often have a unique rusty color on their horns. This is thought to be a result of rubbing against the elephant tree. The ewes' horns are much smaller and lighter. They do not tend to curl. The head and horns of an adult ram may weigh more than 30 pounds. Annual growth rings indicate the animal's age. Both rams and ewes use their horns for fighting and as tools to break open cactus, which they consume.

Rams battle to determine the dominant animal. The winner gains possession of the ewes. Facing each other, rams charge head-on from distances of twenty feet or more. They crash their massive horns together with tremendous impact. They keep this up until one or the other ceases.

Bighorn live in separate ram and ewe bands most of the year. They gather during the breeding season. The breeding season is usually from July through October. Gestation lasts about six months. The lambs are usually born in late winter.

In the late 1800s and early 1900s, bighorn sheep populations rapidly declined. Domestic cattle and sheep, along with wild horses and burros, competed with bighorn, especially at waterholes. Domestic stock also introduced diseases to bighorn populations.

Activities that influence bighorn sheep numbers include disturbance from a wide variety of sources. These include hunting and other recreational uses of their habitat. Poaching is also a problem. Bighorn's habitats are disturbed by roads, fences, mining, and military and recreational activities. Individual bands become isolated. Eventually whole populations of desert bighorn sheep can be lost as their usable habitat becomes increasingly intruded upon by humans.

1. What is the **main** idea of the third paragraph?

   A. The desert bighorn are closely related to domestic sheep.
   B. Padded hooves help the bighorn to escape from predators.
   C. The desert bighorn can survive in places with little water.
   D. Human interference is damaging the bighorn population.

2. Read the sentence below from the passage.

   Bighorn rely on their keen eyesight to detect <u>potential</u> predators.

   In the sentence, the word <u>potential</u> probably means

   A. able.
   B. powerful.
   C. implied.
   D. possible.

3. Rams **probably** charge at each other in order to

   A. gain ewes.
   B. win water.
   C. have fun.
   D. make allies.

4. Which of the following is **probably** the biggest threat to desert bighorn sheep today?

   A. domestic cattle
   B. mountain lions
   C. human activities
   D. wild horses

5. How can we help protect desert bighorn sheep? Identify and explain one way people can help desert bighorn sheep. Use details from the passage to support your answer.

CHILD SAFETY SEATS

BUYING A CHILD SAFETY SEAT

Buy only those child safety seats that meet U.S. Department of Transportation (DOT) requirements. Look for a label that says, "This child restraint system conforms to all applicable federal motor safety standards." The stamp of manufacturing should have been dated after January 1, 1981.

Do not buy a used child safety seat if the instructions or DOT label are missing. You cannot be sure that this seat will provide adequate protection for your child.

Buy a seat that's easy to use.

One important note: Not every child safety seat will fit in every car. Some vehicles' belts may not be compatible. If the car seat you have doesn't work, don't force it or you'll risk a drastic reduction in the car seat's effectiveness. Find a seat that works.

A PARENT'S GUIDE TO PICKING THE APPROPRIATE SAFETY SEAT FOR NEWBORNS, TODDLERS, LITTLE KIDS, AND BIG KIDS

NEWBORNS: from Birth to 9–12 months, or 20 pounds

All newborns must ride in the back seat of the car in rear-facing safety seats. This is the safest position possible for two reasons:

- An infant can be seriously injured or killed by an inflating air bag.
- The driver is less likely to be distracted by the baby while driving.

The car seat should be firmly fastened in place and it shouldn't slide from side to side. Be sure to read the manufacturer's instructions.

At first, when a very young baby can't support its head, you may need to put rolled towels around the head to keep it from flopping forward. Keep the straps over your child's shoulders. Adjust the harness so you can fit only one finger underneath the straps on your child's chest. The chest clip should be even with the child's armpits.

Parents often want to put their new babies in the front seat where they're easier to see. While this may be tempting, don't do it! Remember that putting an infant's rear-facing restraint up front puts the baby directly in the path of the air bag where a serious injury or death could occur if the air bag inflates.

TODDLERS: 9–12 months, or 20 pounds, to 4 years, or 40 pounds

When newborns outgrow their rear-facing restraints, they can graduate to child safety seats that face forward. Like rear-facing seats, these should always be placed in the back seat.

Read the instructions concerning safety seats both from your car owner's manual and from the manufacturer of your safety seat.

Make sure that the straps of the car seat go over your child's shoulder. Straps should be snug enough so you can slip only one finger underneath on your child's chest. Place the chest clip at armpit level.

SMALL CHILDREN: 4 years, or 40 pounds, to 8 years, or 70 pounds

Keep children in convertible or toddler seats as long as they will fit. When they have outgrown the convertible or toddler seat, use a booster seat that positions the lap/shoulder belt correctly. The lap belt should be across the child's hips and the shoulder belt shouldn't cross the face or the front of the neck.

BIG KIDS: 8 years and older, or 70 pounds or more

When a child is tall enough to sit with knees bent at the edge of the seat he or she can use the adult lap/shoulder belt provided in the car. At first, some children may need a special booster seat. Make sure that the seat belt fits properly. Never allow children to put the safety belt shoulder portions behind themselves or under their arms.

There are only two exceptions to putting infants in the back seat: 1) if your car does not have a back seat; 2) if you can deactivate the passenger air bag. If you do deactivate, remember to always reactivate the air bag when preparing to ride with older passengers.

1. In the second paragraph, the word <u>adequate</u> probably means

   A. customary.
   B. artificial.
   C. sufficient.
   D. frequent.

2. According to the passage, why should parents adjust the harness so that only one finger can fit under the straps?

   A. to allow the child to move around in the back seat while driving
   B. to make sure that the harness is tight enough to prevent injury
   C. to make sure that the harness isn't going to break in an accident
   D. to allow the harness to expand with the child as he or she grows

3. How are new safety seats **different** from used safety seats?

   A. New safety seats may not protect children as well as used ones do.
   B. Used safety seats may not come with DOT labels.
   C. Used safety seats may not fit in newer cars.
   D. New safety seats may not come with shoulder straps.

4. Newborns should never be in forward-facing safety seats because

   A. the infants could be at risk of serious injury.
   B. the driver could be inattentive to the baby.
   C. the infants are not able to support their heads.
   D. the driver is not able to read the directions.

5. Write part of a manual for babysitters that tells how to keep children of any age safe in cars. Emphasize the points that you think are **most** important.

"THE CREMATION OF SAM McGEE"

by Robert William Service

There are strange things done in the midnight sun
By the men who moil for gold;
The Arctic trails have their secret tales
That would make your blood run cold;
The Northern Lights have seen queer sights,
But the queerest they ever did see
Was that night on the marge of Lake Lebarge
I cremated Sam McGee.

Now Sam McGee was from Tennessee,
where the cotton blooms and blows.
Why he left his home in the South to roam
'round the Pole, God only knows.
He was always cold, but the land of gold
seemed to hold him like a spell;
Though he'd often say in his homely way
that he'd "sooner live in Hell."

On a Christmas day we were mushing our way
over the Dawson trail.
Talk of your cold! through the parka's fold
it stabbed like a driven nail.
If our eyes we'd close, then the lashes froze
till sometimes we couldn't see,
It wasn't much fun, but the only one
to whimper was Sam McGee.

And that very night, as we lay packed tight
in our robes beneath the snow,
And the dogs were fed, and the stars o'erhead
were dancing heel and toe,
He turned to me, and "Cap," says he,
"I'll cash in this trip, I guess;
And if I do, I'm asking that you
won't refuse my last request."

Well he seemed so low that I couldn't say no;
then he says with a sort of moan,
"It's the cursed cold, and it's got right hold
till I'm chilled clean through to the bone.
Yet 'taint being dead—it's the awful dread
of the icy grave that pains;
So I want you to swear that, foul or fair,
you'll cremate my last remains."

A pal's last need is a thing to heed.
so I swore I would not fail;
And we started on at the streak of dawn;
but God! he looked ghastly pale.
He crouched on the sleigh, and he raved all day
of his home in Tennessee;
And before nightfall a corpse was all
that was left of Sam McGee.

There wasn't a breath in that land of death,
and I hurried, horror-driven,
With a corpse half hid that I couldn't get rid,
because of a promise given;
It was lashed to the sleigh, and it seemed to say:
"You may tax your brawn and brains,
But you promised true, and it's up to you
to cremate these last remains."

Now a promise made is a debt unpaid,
the trail has its own stern code,
In the days to come, though my lips were dumb
in my heart how I cursed that load!
In the long, long night, by the lone firelight,
while the huskies, round in a ring,
Howled out their woes to the homeless snows—
Oh God, how I loathed the thing!

And every day that quiet clay
seemed to heavy and heavier grow;
And on I went, though the dogs were spent
and the grub was getting low.
The trail was bad, and I felt half mad,
but I swore I would not give in;
And I'd often sing to the hateful thing,
and it hearkened with a grin.

Till I came to the marge of Lake Lebarge,
and a derelict there lay;
It was jammed in the ice, but I saw in a trice
it was called the *Alice May*,
And I looked at it, and I thought a bit,
and I looked at my frozen chum;
Then "Here," said I, with a sudden cry,
"is my cre-ma-tor-e-um"!

Some planks I tore from the cabin floor
and I lit the boiler fire;
Some coal I found that was lying around,
and I heaped the fuel higher;
The flames just soared, and the furnace roared
such a blaze you seldom see,
And I burrowed a hole in the glowing coal,
and I stuffed in Sam McGee.

Then I made a hike, for I didn't like
to hear him sizzle so;
And the heavens scowled, and the huskies howled,
and the wind began to blow,
It was icy cold, but the hot sweat rolled
down my cheeks, and I don't know why;
And the greasy smoke in an inky cloak
went streaking down the sky.

I do not know how long in the snow
I wrestled with grisly fear;
But the stars came out and they danced about
ere again I ventured near;
I was sick with dread, but I bravely said,
"I'll just take a peep inside.
I guess he's cooked, and it's time I looked".
Then the door I opened wide.

And there sat Sam, looking cool and calm,
in the heart of the furnace roar;
And he wore a smile you could see a mile,
and he said, "Please close that door.
It's fine in here, but I greatly fear
you'll let in the cold and storm—
Since I left Plumtree, down in Tennessee,
it's the first time I've been warm."

There are strange things done in the midnight sun
By the men who moil for gold;
The Arctic trails have their secret tales
That would make your blood run cold;
The Northern Lights have seen queer sights,
But the queerest they ever did see
Was that night on the marge of Lake Lebarge
I cremated Sam McGee.

1. What was Sam McGee afraid of?

   A. dying before the end of the trip
   B. resting in a cold grave
   C. never finding gold
   D. lying in a fiery furnace

2. In the second line, the word <u>moil</u> means

   A. mail.
   B. melt.
   C. labor.
   D. trade.

3. Which **best** describes how the speaker feels about traveling with Sam McGee's body?

   A. scared, but content
   B. troubled, but determined
   C. excited, but uncomfortable
   D. pleased, but mournful

4. Read the line below from the poem.

   It stabbed like a driven nail . . .

   The line contains an example of which type of figurative language?

   A. simile
   B. metaphor
   C. personification
   D. onomatopoeia

5. What is the speaker's **major** conflict in the poem?

   A. He must keep a difficult promise to his friend.
   B. He must find his way through the snow.
   C. He must decide what to do with the gold he has found.
   D. He must race to keep Sam McGee alive.

6. Why did Sam McGee **probably** stay in the Arctic?

   A. He liked the climate.
   B. He grew up there.
   C. He loved the cold.
   D. He wanted gold.

7. The author's **main** purpose for writing the poem is to

   A. warn.
   B. teach.
   C. entertain.
   D. persuade.

8. Explain what happened to Sam McGee. Include three important details from his life.

WEST INDIAN MANATEE

The West Indian manatee is a large gray or brown aquatic mammal. Adults average about 10 feet in length. They weigh 1,000 pounds. They have no hind limbs. Their forelimbs are modified as flippers. Manatee tails are flattened horizontally and rounded. Their body is covered with sparse hairs. Their muzzles have stiff whiskers.

Manatees will consume any aquatic vegetation available. They sometimes even eat shoreline vegetation. They are primarily herbivorous. They will occasionally feed on fish. Manatees may spend about five hours a day feeding. They consume four to nine percent of their body weight a day.

Manatee cows usually bear a single calf. Calves reach sexual maturity at three to six years of age. Mature females may give birth every two to five years. The only long-term, stable bond among manatees is the one between a cow and her calf. Weaning occurs between nine and 24 months of age. A cow and calf may continue to associate with each other for several more years.

During the winter months, the United States' manatee population confines itself to the coastal waters of southern Florida. They also can be found in springs and warm water outlets as far north as southeastern Georgia. During the summer months, they may migrate as far north as coastal Virginia. They also can be found on the Louisiana coast of the Gulf of Mexico.

The population of manatees in Florida has been estimated to be at least 1,865 individuals. In the last decade, mortality in Florida has averaged nearly 150 animals a year. This is double that of the preceding decade. The average proportion of first-year calves in the population is 10 percent with a range of five to 15 percent.

Manatees inhabit both salt water and fresh water of sufficient depth throughout their range. They may be encountered in canals, rivers, estuarine habitats, and saltwater bays. On occasion they have been observed as far as 3.7 miles off the Florida Gulf coast.

1. What do manatees eat?

   A. plants
   B. meat
   C. fish
   D. sand

2. Which of these **best** describes manatees?

A. small fish
B. large fish
C. small mammals
D. large mammals

3. Why do you think twice as many manatees now die each year as happened 10 years ago? Use details from the passage to support your answer.

I think predator pop is increasing

ALFRED VAIL AND THE TELEGRAPH

Alfred Vail was born in 1807. He was a son of Judge Stephen Vail. Stephen Vail was the master of the Speedwell Iron Works at Morristown, New Jersey. After Alfred finished village school, his father took him into the Works.

In 1832, Alfred went to the University of the City of New York. He graduated in October 1836. While he was still in doubt about his future, he chanced to see the telegraph. That decided him. About this experience he wrote:

3 I accidentally and without invitation called upon Professor Morse at the University. Professor Morse was exhibiting an apparatus. He called it his "Electro-Magnetic Telegraph." There were wires suspended in the room running from one end of it to the other, and returning many times, making a length of seventeen hundred feet. The two ends of the wire were connected with an electro-magnet fastened to a vertical wooden frame. In front of the magnet was its armature, and also a wooden lever or arm fitted at its extremity to hold a lead-pencil. . . . I saw this instrument work, and became thoroughly acquainted with the principle of its operation. I was struck with the rude machine containing, as I believed, the germ of what was destined to produce great changes in the conditions and relations of mankind. I well recollect the impression which was then made upon my mind. I rejoiced to think that I lived in such a day. My mind contemplated the future in which so grand and mighty an agent was about to be introduced for the benefit of the world. Before leaving the room in which I beheld for the first time this magnificent invention, I asked Professor Morse if he intended to make an experiment on a more extended line of conductors. He replied that he did. He desired pecuniary assistance to carry out his plans. I promised him assistance provided he would admit me into a share of the invention, to which proposition he assented. I then returned to my boarding-house, locked the door of my room, threw myself upon the bed. I gave myself up to reflection upon the mighty results that were certain to follow the introduction of this new agent in meeting and serving the wants of the world. With the atlas in my hand I traced the most important lines which would most certainly be erected in the United States, and calculated their length. The question then rose in my mind, whether the electro-magnet could be made to work through the necessary lengths of line. After much reflection I came to the conclusion that, provided the magnet would work even at a distance of eight or ten miles, there could be no risk in embarking in the enterprise. And upon this I decided in my own mind to SINK OR SWIM WITH IT.

Young Vail applied to his father for financial assistance for his professor, Samuel Morse. Judge Stephen Vail was a man of enterprise and intelligence. He had forged the shaft of the *Savannah*, the first steamship to cross the Atlantic. Morse was invited to Speedwell with his apparatus, so that the judge might see it for himself. Two thousand dollars was required to procure the patents and to construct an instrument to bring before the Congress. In spite of a financial depression, the judge was brave enough to lend his assistance.

On September 23, 1837, an agreement was signed between the inventor and Alfred Vail. Vail was to construct, at his own expense, a model for exhibition to a committee of Congress. In return Vail was to receive one-fourth of the patent rights in the country. Provision was made also to give Vail an interest in any foreign patents which he might furnish the means to obtain. Morse obtained the American patent on October 3, 1837.

For many months, Alfred Vail worked in a secret room at the iron factory making the new model. When the workshop was rebuilt later on, this room was preserved as a memorial of the telegraph, for it was here that the true Morse instrument, such as we know it, was constructed.

The first machine made at Speedwell was a copy of that devised by Morse. As Vail grew more intimate with the subject his own ingenuity came into play, and he soon improved on the original. The pencil was discarded for a fountain pen, and the zigzag signals for the short and long lines now termed dots and dashes.

8 This important alteration led him to the "Morse alphabet," or code of signals, by which a letter is transmitted as a group of short and long jets, indicated as *dots* and *dashes* on the paper. Thus the letter E, which is so common in English words, is now transmitted by a short jet which makes a *dot*; T, another common letter, by a long jet, making a *dash*; and Q, a rare letter, by the group *dash, dash, dot, dash*. Vail tried to compute the relative frequency of all the letters in order to arrange his alphabet. A happy idea enabled him to save his time. He went to the office of the local newspaper. There he found the result he wanted in the type-cases of the compositors. At present the Morse—or, rather, Vail—code is the universal telegraphic code of symbols.

1. In paragraph 3, what does Alfred Vail mean when he says that the machine contained "the germ of what was destined to produce great changes in the conditions and relations of mankind"?

   A. He was afraid that he would get sick if he helped Professor Morse.
   B. He felt that the machine would cause many problems for Professor Morse.
   C. He believed that the machine was the beginning of something important.
   D. He thought that he could make a lot of money by helping Professor Morse.

2. What was the biggest improvement that Alfred Vail made to Professor Morse's machine?

   A. He replaced the pencil Morse used with a fountain pen.
   B. He used metal instead of wood for the machine's parts.
   C. He created a new code of signals for the machine to use.
   D. He made a much larger version of Morse's machine.

3. What does the word <u>transmitted</u> mean in paragraph 8?

   A. organized
   B. worked
   C. made
   D. sent

4. Why did the author most likely write this passage?

   A. to tell readers how to use Morse code
   B. to explain how the telegraph was completed
   C. to describe what Alfred Vail's life was like
   D. to inform readers of new inventions

5. Think about how Alfred Vail felt about the telegraph.

   - With all the technology we have today, what sort of invention would impress you as much as the telegraph impressed Alfred Vail?

   Use information from the passage to support your response.

DELAWARE WATER GAP

Delaware Water Gap has habitats ranging from rivers and ponds to dry ridge tops. Delaware Water Gap is home to a wide variety of animals. They range from black bears weighing up to eight hundred pounds to ruby-throated hummingbirds, measuring only three to four inches long.

The Delaware River and its tributaries are home to more than sixty fish species. That includes both migratory species and species that make the park their permanent home. The migratory species include eels and American shad. They travel between the upper reaches of the river and the Atlantic Ocean.

Great blue and green-backed herons wade in shallows. They are looking for fish, frogs, and crustaceans for a meal. Otters glide silently through the water. On the river's flood plain, rich soil supports bountiful farm fields. Visitors can commonly see white-tailed deer and wild turkey searching for food. After nightfall, the park comes alive with a whole new set of animals. Foxes, coyotes, bobcats and raccoons roam. In the night sky are owls and six species of bats.

Delaware Water Gap National Recreation Area is blessed with a variety of habitats. They are suitable for many types of mammals. Under the leaf litter, you may find mice and shrews. In more open areas look for groundhogs, cottontail rabbits, weasels, skunks, red fox, coyotes and white-tailed deer. Along the waterways look for raccoons, muskrats, mink, and beavers. If you are lucky enough, you might even see some otters frolicking along the bank. In the forest, look for gray squirrels (some are jet black), gray fox, and black bears. At dusk, look up to see flying squirrels gliding their way from tree to tree.

5 The area boasts twenty-five species of frogs, toads and salamanders. They live or breed in the park's <u>diverse</u> aquatic and wetland habitats. Visitors may glimpse a red-backed salamander, or perhaps the northern dusky salamander, under a rotting log. On rainy nights in late winter, look for wood frogs and spotted salamanders crossing roads on their way to breeding ponds. Later on, a deafening chorus of spring peepers will announce spring's arrival. With the coming of warmer weather and longer days, visitors to any of the park's lakes or ponds are sure to hear the bellow of the bullfrog.

The park is home to sixteen species of snakes. There are eight species of turtles and two kinds of lizards. As with amphibians, many suffer population declines from habitat loss or fragmentation, illegal collection, and commercial exploitation. Of the park's twenty-six species, eight are of "special concern" in one or both states (Pennsylvania or New Jersey). One species—the bog turtle—is protected under the Endangered Species Act.

Commonly encountered reptiles include painted turtles and water snakes. In warm weather, both can often be spotted at one of the park's old farm ponds. The turtle is basking on a floating log. The snake is draped over the branches of a shoreline shrub.

Look for garter and ribbon snakes in adjacent wetlands.

Paddlers on the Delaware River should keep a keen eye out for map turtles, which quietly slip off their basking rocks on close approach. All too often, our reptilian encounters are with road kills. Avoid contributing to this increasingly serious problem by observing speed limits on all of the park's roadways. Turtles and snakes may travel long distances to and from their feeding, nesting, and hibernation sites. Road crossings take their toll. Among the least frequently encountered reptiles are the lizards and venomous snakes. Small populations of five-lined skinks, northern fence lizards, northern copperheads, and timber rattlesnakes all inhabit the park.

The park is a mosaic of landforms further altered by centuries of human activities. These diverse landscapes provide habitat for a variety of birds that breed here or migrate through. More than 260 species have been identified in the area.

River and stream corridors are hosts to species ranging from Louisiana water thrush to bald eagles. Bottomland forests along the river support cerulean warblers. Hemlock-dominated ravines offer breeding habitat for blackburnian and black-throated green warblers, acadian flycatchers, and hermit thrush.

Agricultural fields provide open space that is frequented by wild turkey. The surrounding trees offer hunting perches for raptors scanning fields for small prey.

Grasslands provide breeding habitat for bobolink and grasshopper sparrow. Waterfowl, shorebirds, and herons inhabit wetlands. Deciduous forests, perhaps the largest landscape component, provide habitat for birds ranging from the scarlet tanager to the ruffed grouse.

During the fall and spring months many birds migrate along the river valley. More than thirty species of warblers have been recorded during spring migration.

In the fall the Kittatinny Ridge provides an important migratory corridor for raptors. The Delaware River valley offers an important wintering habitat for a large population of bald eagles. They are attracted to the open water for foraging. Golden eagles are less frequently sighted but some are recorded nearly every winter. Bald eagles are frequently seen along the river during the summer months.

1. What is this article mostly about?

   A. migratory birds that stop in the Delaware Water Gap
   B. different animals found throughout the Delaware Water Gap
   C. activities in which visitors to the Delaware Water Gap can take part
   D. animals that live in the forest habitat of the Delaware Water Gap

2. Which group of animals exhibits the highest number of different species found in the Delaware Water Gap?

   A. frogs
   B. birds
   C. fish
   D. snakes

3. What is the most likely reason that you would not see a bog turtle while exploring the Delaware Water Gap?

   A. They are very shy around people.
   B. They hide beneath the leaves of the forest.
   C. They are an endangered species.
   D. They spend much of their time underwater.

4. In paragraph 5, diverse means

   A. clean.
   B. various.
   C. protected.
   D. widespread.

5. In which habitat of the Delaware Water Gap would you most likely find a wild turkey?

   A. a deciduous forest
   B. an agricultural field
   C. a dry ridge top
   D. a wetland

6. The purpose of this article is to

   A. entertain readers with stories about animals that live in the Delaware Water Gap.
   B. persuade readers to consider taking a vacation to the Delaware Water Gap.
   C. encourage readers to participate in efforts to protect the Delaware Water Gap.
   D. inform readers of the habitats and animals in the Delaware Water Gap.

7. The MOST prevalent habitat in the Delaware Water Gap is

   A. deciduous forest.
   B. floodplain.
   C. grassland.
   D. wetland.

8. Name three different animals that inhabit the park. State where and when each can most likely be spotted.

9. Imagine and describe a visit to the Delaware Water Gap.

AN ACCOUNT OF THE STILL FAMILY HISTORY

Written by Dr. James Still

I was born in Washington Township, Burlington County, State of New Jersey, April ninth, one thousand eight hundred and twelve, at what was called the Indian Mill. . . . My father's name was Levin Still, and my mother's name was Charity. They were born in Maryland, and were slaves. My father bought his freedom, and then undertook to free his wife by bringing her to New Jersey. . . .

My mother . . . was born a slave, and in slavery reared to womanhood. Four children were born to her in her time of servitude, two sons and two daughters. Her anxious spirit longed for freedom. No way presented itself but that of flight, and escape by flight she effected at a convenient season, leaving two little boys in bondage, and taking with her two little daughters. She fled to New Jersey, and took up her abode there. Often did she have cause to tremble for fear of her old taskmaster, well knowing that the law was against her, and he had a right by the laws of her country to claim her and her children, and carry them back to slavery. . . .

The loss of the two little boys left behind in slavery was a great grief. She frequently spoke of them, and wondered where they were, whether dead or alive. Forty-five years rolled away, and bore her long-absent son Peter to her arms again. . . . He served in slavery, . . . and by saving and industry was enabled to buy his freedom of his master whilst living in Alabama. Having purchased his freedom, he set out toward the North to look for his relations, of whom he knew nothing, and had heard nothing from the time he was five years old. He came to Philadelphia in eighteen hundred and fifty, found his own brother was a clerk in the Anti-Slavery office there, and from him learned the whereabouts of his mother and brothers. From thence he came to my house, and we took him to see our mother. . . . After spending a little time among the relatives whom he had never before met, he made up his mind to try to relieve the family whom he had left behind in slavery.

He set his face southward, and reaching Alabama, told his wife and children of his success in the North, and set about planning to release them. . . . He bade them a hopeful farewell and came North to consult friends. . . . Some counseled one way and some another. . . .

5 A gentleman finally volunteered to go and bring his family to him. This person reached Alabama, found those whom he was seeking, and succeeded in conveying them several hundred miles on their way North. He was overtaken, however, by their master, who captured them, carried the slaves back to bondage, and killed the man who had generously volunteered to risk his life in their behalf.

Peter, at hearing this news, was nearly heartbroken. He next proposed to collect money to purchase his wife and children. After traveling about for five years, he gathered the sum of five thousand dollars with which he bought them. . . . They were delivered to him in eighteen hundred and fifty-five, the wife, two sons, and a daughter. They arrived at my house on January thirteenth of that year, and after showing his family to anxious friends who were interested, Peter settled down with them in Burlington, New Jersey.

—from *Early Recollections and Life of Dr. James Still (1877)*

1. What did Peter do after purchasing his freedom?

   A. He traveled to the North to look for his family.
   B. He fled to New Jersey and bought a home there.
   C. He went to the South to spend time with his friends.
   D. He volunteered to help other slaves find freedom.

2. Why did the author most likely write this passage?

   A. to explain the horrors faced by slaves
   B. to describe his life and the lives of his family members
   C. to inform readers of New Jersey's slave laws
   D. to entertain readers with a story about a close family

3. What happened to the man who tried to help Peter save his family?

   A. He was taken as a slave in Alabama.
   B. He never found Peter's wife and children.
   C. He was killed by a slave master.
   D. He became great friends with Peter.

4. Who is telling the story in this passage?

   A. a first-person narrator
   B. a third-person narrator
   C. Peter Still
   D. Levin Still

5. In paragraph 5, <u>bondage</u> means

   A. servitude.
   B. prison.
   C. travel.
   D. home.

6. Why do you think the "gentleman" risked his life for Peter's family?

AN EYEWITNESS ACCOUNT OF THE BATTLE OF TRENTON – Part I

by an officer on Washington's staff

New Town, Pennsylvania, December 22, 1776

Things have been going against us since last August. We were forced to give up Long Island. We lost three thousand men and a great amount of supplies. In October we were forced to evacuate New York and cross the Hudson into New Jersey. We reached Trenton on December 2nd. It was prudent forethought on the part of General Washington to send General Maxwell ahead to secure all the boats on the Delaware River and to have them at Trenton upon our arrival. If it had not been done we should have been in a bad fix with Cornwallis at our heels. As it was, the Hessians under Count Donop and Colonel Rahl arrived in that village in season to fire a few shots at the last boat. According to the last accounts, General Howe and General Cornwallis have gone to New York. They left General Grant with a few hundred English troops at Princeton, Colonel Rahl with fifteen hundred Hessians at Trenton and Count Donop with two thousand at Bordentown, ten miles down the river from Trenton.

Washington's headquarters are here in this little village of New Town. It is back from the river northwest of Trenton. General Greene and General Sullivan, with their divisions, numbering twenty-five hundred men and sixteen cannon, are ten miles upstream at McConkey's Ferry. A portion of the boats are there. General Ewing, with two thousand men, is on this side of the river a little below Trenton. General Cadwallader and General Putnam are at Bristol, ten miles further down, with as many more.

3 I rode along the river yesterday morning and could see the Hessians in Trenton. It is a pretty village, containing about one hundred thirty houses and a Presbyterian meetinghouse. A stone bridge spans the Assunpink Creek on the road leading to Bordentown. There are apple orchards and gardens. Rahl has his own regiment and Knyphausen a few dragoons and fifty riflemen. The Hessians call them "Yagers." He has six cannon. Knyphausen has two of them, two stand in front of Rahl's headquarters, and two up by the Pennington road. A scout just in says that General Howe has issued a proclamation, offering pardon to everybody in New Jersey who will lay down their arms and take the oath of allegiance. He says that Howe and Cornwallis are well satisfied with what they have accomplished. Cornwallis is going to England to tell the King that the <u>rebellion</u> is about over. Howe is going to have a good time in New York attending dinner parties. From what I see I am quite

certain Washington intends to make some movement soon. He keeps his own counsel, but is very much determined.

December 23—Orders have been issued to cook rations for three days. Washington has just given the countersign, "Victory or Death." He has written a letter to General Cadwallader at Bristol, which he has entrusted to me to copy. He intends to cross the river, make a ten-mile march to Trenton, and attack Rahl just before daybreak. Ewing is to cross and seize the bridge crossing the Assunpink. Putnam and Cadwallader are to cross and make a feint of attacking Donop so that he cannot hasten to Rahl's assistance.

December 24—A scout just in says that the Hessians have a picket on the Pennington road half a mile out from Trenton, and another at Dickenson's house, on the river road.

1. "An Eyewitness Account of the Battle of Trenton" is specifically about

   A. George Washington's time in the army.
   B. one soldier's experience during a battle.
   C. where the armies traveled in New Jersey.
   D. George Washington becoming president.

2. In paragraph 3, <u>rebellion</u> means

   A. occasion.
   B. uprising.
   C. blizzard.
   D. holiday.

3. The soldier thinks that Washington is going to

   A. inform the soldiers of his plans.
   B. let another general lead his troops.
   C. move to attack the enemy's camp.
   D. tell the soldiers that they are free to go.

4. The soldier copies a letter that talks about Washington's plans to attack the enemy on the morning of December 25th.

   - Give TWO reasons why you think that this is a good plan or a bad one.
   - How do you think the soldier feels about this plan?

   Use information from the article to support your response.

AN EYEWITNESS ACCOUNT OF THE BATTLE OF TRENTON - Part II

by an officer on Washington's staff

December 25—Christmas morning. They make a great deal of Christmas in Germany, and no doubt the Hessians will drink a great deal of beer and have a dance to-night. They will be sleepy tomorrow morning. Washington will set the tune for them about daybreak. The rations are cooked. New flints and ammunition have been distributed. Colonel [John] Glover's fishermen from Marblehead, Massachusetts, are to manage the boats just as they did in the retreat from Long Island.

Christmas, 6 p.m—The regiments have had their evening parade, but instead of returning to their quarters are marching toward the ferry. It is fearfully cold and raw and a snowstorm is setting in. The wind is northeast and beats in the faces of the men. It will be a terrible night for the soldiers who have no shoes. Some of them have tied old rags around their feet; others are barefoot, but I have not heard a man complain. They are ready to suffer any hardship and die rather than give up their liberty. I have just copied the order for marching. Both divisions are to go from the ferry to Bear Tavern, two miles. They will separate there; Washington will accompany Greene's division with a part of the artillery down the Pennington road; Sullivan and the rest of the artillery will take the river road.

December 26, 3 a.m.—I am writing in the ferry house. The troops are all over, and the boats have gone back for the artillery. We are three hours behind the set time. Glover's men have had a hard time to force the boats through the floating ice with the snow drifting in their faces. I never have seen Washington so determined as he is now. He stands on the bank of the river, wrapped in his cloak, superintending the landing of his troops. He is calm and collected, but very determined. The storm is changing to sleet, and cuts like a knife. The last cannon is being landed, and we are ready to mount our horses.

December 26, Noon—It was nearly 4 o'clock, when we started. The two divisions divided at Bear Tavern.

At Birmingham, three and a half miles south of the tavern, a man came with a message from General Sullivan that the storm was wetting the muskets and rendering them unfit for service. "Tell General Sullivan," said Washington, "to use the bayonet. I am resolved to take Trenton."

It was broad daylight when we came to a house where a man was chopping wood. He was very much surprised when he saw us. "Can you tell me where the Hessian picket is?" Washington asked. The man hesitated, but I said, "You need not be frightened, it is General Washington who asks the question." His face brightened and he pointed toward the house of Mr. Howell.

1. Why does the soldier believe that the Germans will be sleepy?

   A. It will be hard to sleep in the rain.
   B. They will be tired from the battle.
   C. They will stay up late celebrating.
   D. It will be hard to sleep inside a tent.

2. During the attack, what was the biggest problem for many of the soldiers?

   A. It was raining hard.
   B. It was very dark out.
   C. They had little food.
   D. They had no shoes.

3. In the last paragraph, <u>the man hesitated</u> before giving them information. This tells the reader that the man

   A. was afraid that he would be taken prisoner.
   B. wanted to keep the information to himself.
   C. did not know where the enemy was staying.
   D. did not know he was talking to Washington.

4. Washington planned to attack the Germans on December 25.

   - Describe the weather conditions that the soldiers faced.
   - Do you think Washington was discouraged by the weather? Give TWO reasons to explain your answer.

   Use information from the article to support your response.

AN EYEWITNESS ACCOUNT OF THE BATTLE OF TRENTON – Part III

by an officer on Washington's staff

It was just 8 o'clock. Looking down the road I saw a Hessian running out from the house. He yelled in Dutch [German] and swung his arms. Three or four others came out with their guns. Two of them fired at us, but the bullets whistled over our heads. Some of General [Adam] Stephen's men rushed forward and captured two. The other took to their heels, running toward Mr. [Alexander] Calhoun's house, where the picket guard was stationed, about twenty men under Captain Altenbrockum. They came running out of the house. The Captain flourished his sword and tried to form his men. Some of them fired at us; others ran toward the village. The next moment we heard drums beat and a bugle sound, and then from the west came the boom of a cannon. General Washington's face lighted up instantly, for he knew that it was one of Sullivan's guns. We could see a great commotion down toward the meetinghouse, men running here and there, officers swinging their swords, artillerymen harnessing their horses. Captain [Thomas] Forrest unlimbered his guns. Washington gave the order to advance, and rushed on the junction of King and Queen Streets. Forrest wheeled six of his cannon into position to sweep both streets. The riflemen under Colonel [Edward] Hand and [Charles] Scott's and [Robert] Lawson's battalions went upon the run through the fields on the left just ready to open fire with two of their cannon when Captain [William] Washington and Lieutenant [James] Monroe with their men rushed forward and captured them. We saw Rahl come riding up the street from his headquarters, which were at Stacy Potts' house. We could hear him shouting in Dutch, "My brave soldiers, advance." His men were frightened and confused, for our men were firing upon them from fences and houses and they were falling fast. Instead of advancing they ran into an apple orchard. The officers tried to rally them, but our men kept advancing and picking off the officers. It was not long before Rahl tumbled from his horse and his soldiers threw down their guns and gave themselves up as prisoners.

While this was taking place on the Pennington road, Colonel John Stark, from New Hampshire, in the advance on the river road was driving Knyphausen's men pell-mell through the town. Sullivan sent a portion of his troops under [Brigadier-General Arthur] St. Clair to seize the bridge and cut off the retreat of the Hessians toward Bordentown. Sullivan's men shot the artillery horses and captured two cannon attached to Knyphausen's regiment.

December 26, 3 p.m— . . . We have taken nearly 1000 prisoners, six cannon, more than 1000 muskets, twelve drums, and four colors. About forty Hessians were killed or wounded. Our loss is only two killed and three wounded . . . .

I have just been with General Washington and Greene to see Rahl. He will not live through the night. He asked that his men might be kindly treated. Washington promised that he would see they were well cared for.

December 27, 1776—Here we are back in our camp with the prisoners and trophies. Washington is keeping his promise; the soldiers are in the New Town Meetinghouse and other buildings. He has just given directions for tomorrow's dinner. All the captured Hessian officers are to dine with him. He bears the Hessians no malice, but says they have been sold by their Grand Duke to King George and sent to America, when—if they could have their own way—they would be peaceably living in their own country.

It is a glorious victory. It will rejoice the hearts of our friends everywhere and give new life to our hitherto waning fortunes. Washington has baffled the enemy in his retreat from New York. He has pounced upon the Hessians like an eagle upon a hen and is safe once more on this side of the river. If he does nothing more he will live in history as a great military commander.

1. In paragraph 1, <u>commotion</u> means

   A. explosion.
   B. confusion.
   C. building.
   D. gathering.

2. The Americans took over a bridge in order to

   A. keep the Germans from getting help.
   B. have some way for them to escape.
   C. keep the Germans from retreating.
   D. have a place to keep their cannons.

3. The soldiers are amazed by Washington's victory.

- Do you agree with the writer's conclusion about Washington?
- Why or why not?

Use information from the article to support your response.

MARÍA DeCASTRO BLAKE

María DeCastro Blake was born in Vieques, Puerto Rico in 1911. She was the daughter of Francisco DeCastro. He was a fisherman from Cabo Rojo. Her mother was Clotilde Smaine. She was a cook from Vieques.

María grew up in Vieques under the care of her mother. In 1932, María emigrated to New York City. It was shortly after her mother died. María was a high school graduate. She looked for office work. She did not have much knowledge of English. She was only able to get a menial job. It was in the garment industry.

María was determined to improve her life. She began taking English classes at night. She gained skills in the language. She was able to find a secretarial job in Wall Street. She enrolled herself in night courses at Columbia University.

With earnings from her secretarial work, María brought her sisters to New York. In 1942, she married Thomas Blake. He was a native of Jersey City. She had three children. They moved to East Orange, New Jersey in the late 1940s.

In New Jersey, María began to volunteer her time at Saint Patrick's Church. It is in Newark. She began to teach English to Puerto Rican families. They had begun to settle in the city. She tutored the children in the afternoons. In the evenings she taught the adults.

María's husband died in 1960. She took a full-time secretarial job at Rutgers University in Newark. At Rutgers, she worked with the Alumni Office to partner with St. Patrick's. They helped to send poor city children to camp. She explained that she was particularly interested in this project because the children selected were also given free medical exams.

As a staff member of Rutgers, María also promoted the idea of enrolling Hispanic students at the Newark Campus. She convinced the admissions officers at Rutgers that these students deserved a chance. She sought out the parents and urged the students to apply. She helped the students to fill out the applications and financial aid forms. At times she even gave money to those whose checks were late or fell short. Many went on to become professionals. They proudly state that without María Blake's help they could not have succeeded. To them, María was affectionately known as "the Dean."

When Rutgers promoted her to the post of Assistant Dean of Admissions in 1965, María went on to recruit hundreds of Hispanic students. She also sought scholarship funds and internships from government agencies and corporations for the students she recruited. She served both the university and the Hispanic community for twenty-four years.

9 In 1984, María retired. Hundreds attended the ceremony. Dozens paid homage to the woman who had helped them obtain the college education she had been unable to secure for herself.

María's activism in New Jersey led her to collaborate in the establishment of many organizations. Among them were Aspira of New Jersey (Association for the Professional Education of Puerto Ricans), the Puerto Rican Congress, and the Black and Puerto Rican Coalition.

Once retired, she moved back to New York City. There she volunteered her services every week to the New York Public Library and to the Museum of Natural History. She did this for the next seventeen years. María DeCastro Blake only stopped shortly before she died in July 2001. Her legs could not carry her any more.

1. In the article, the author attempts to

   A. tell an adventure story about a girl in Puerto Rico.
   B. challenge an accepted opinion about immigrants.
   C. complain about immigrants coming to America.
   D. explain the life of a woman who helped others.

2. María wanted to send poor city children to camp because the children

   A. could not speak English.
   B. would be educated in camp.
   C. would get medical exams.
   D. were friends of María's.

3. In paragraph 9, the author writes that "dozens paid homage to the woman" who had made their educations possible. What is the meaning of <u>homage</u>?

   A. respect
   B. anger
   C. money
   D. schooling

4. In the first paragraph, why does the author tell about María's early life?

   A. to show that she had a humble background
   B. to explain what life was like in Puerto Rico
   C. to encourage people to visit Puerto Rico
   D. to introduce paragraphs about her parents

5. Hundreds of people attended María DeCastro Blake's retirement ceremony.

   - What did María do throughout her life?
   - How did her actions win her many friends?

   Use information from the article to support your response.

NOTES

NOTES

NOTES

97805701R00109

Made in the USA
Columbia, SC
18 June 2018